FOREWORD BY UMBRA TOY PHOTOS

Well, here we are once again! If you've had the privilege of reading the first volume in this series you'll know exactly what to expect from this book, so at this point I suppose you can just stop reading…but if you'll indulge me a little further I'd like to just say a few things.

When 'Stop Wars: A collection of photos produced by over 50 Toy Photographers from across the globe' (catchy title I know!) was released a while back, I had absolutely no idea just how much attention it would garner, and just how successful it would become. Now, don't get me wrong, the sheer amount of talent on display, and the pure passion and creativity poured into each and every photo was clear to see. It warmed my heart to see so many people embracing the cause, and opening themselves up to our little slice of the photography community.

I'm hoping that we can capture that lightning in a bottle once again with our latest release, and just like the first book, the calibre of photography on display is simply excellent. We've got some of the most talented toy photographers from around the globe, right here in this book, people who didn't have to share their photos, but instead chose to, in order that we might help a worthy cause. It's truly moving to see a community such as this come together, unite around a common goal, and choose to do something.

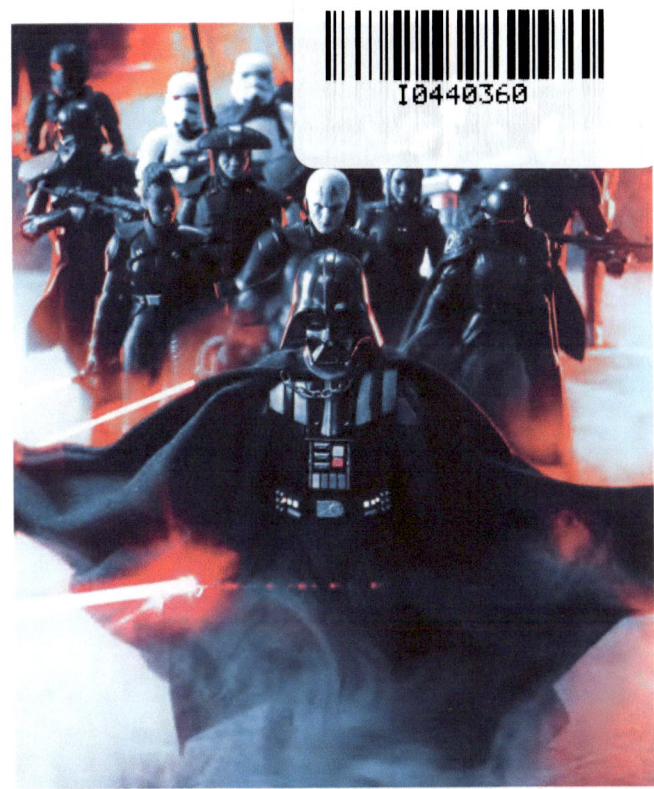

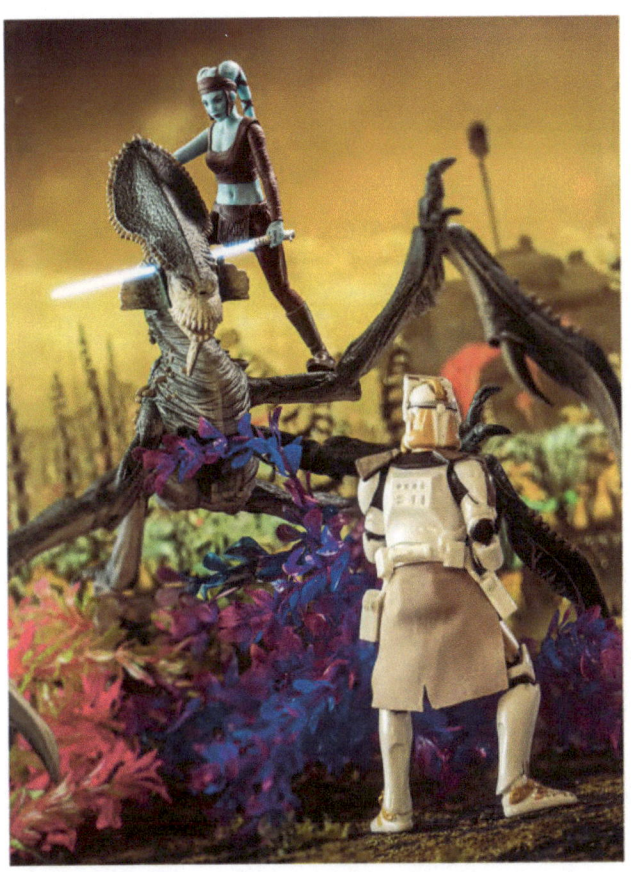

Throughout my few years participating in the toy photography community, one thing has become abundantly clear to me - this is a community who not only loves to help tell a story, they also love to help others tell their stories. There is a true sense of camaraderie, and a real feeling that others go out of their way to help in any way they can, whether it be projects like this book, or giving advice on all things photography related. I've even seen fundraisers for fellow photographers who have fallen on hard times, and that is the essence of what being in the toy photography community is all about.

If you read this book and think to yourself "This toy photography stuff seems pretty cool", well I've got news for you, first of all, yes, I agree, it is cool, but secondly, it's ridiculously easy to start participating yourself. If you have any sort of camera at all, digital camera, phone camera, gameboy camera (maybe?), and some action figures, you've got everything you need to get started. Speaking for myself, I didn't have a clue where to start when I first started doing toy photography, but luckily there are so many amazing tutorials, guides, and videos, readily available online, which I encourage you to view. Who knows, maybe you'll be featured in the next edition of this book?

Enjoy the book, have fun, spread the word, and above all, thank you for supporting this project!

Umbra Toy Photos

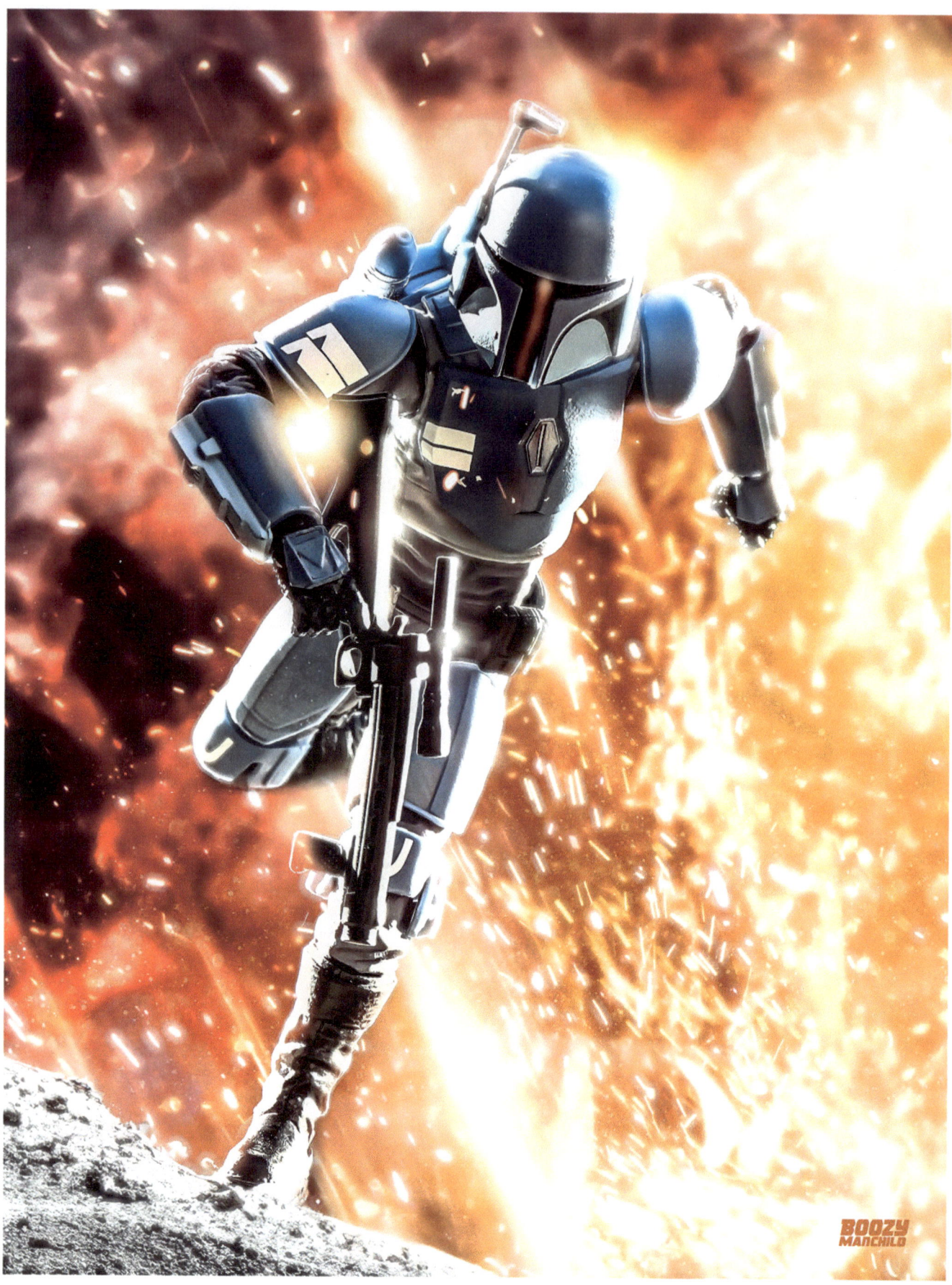

I'm a big fan of The Mandalorian in general, but this is definitely one of my favourite figures from the Black Series line. I had a lot of fun shooting this outside in my back garden! A mixture of practical effects and photoshop work have been used to produce this final image. - @boozymanchild

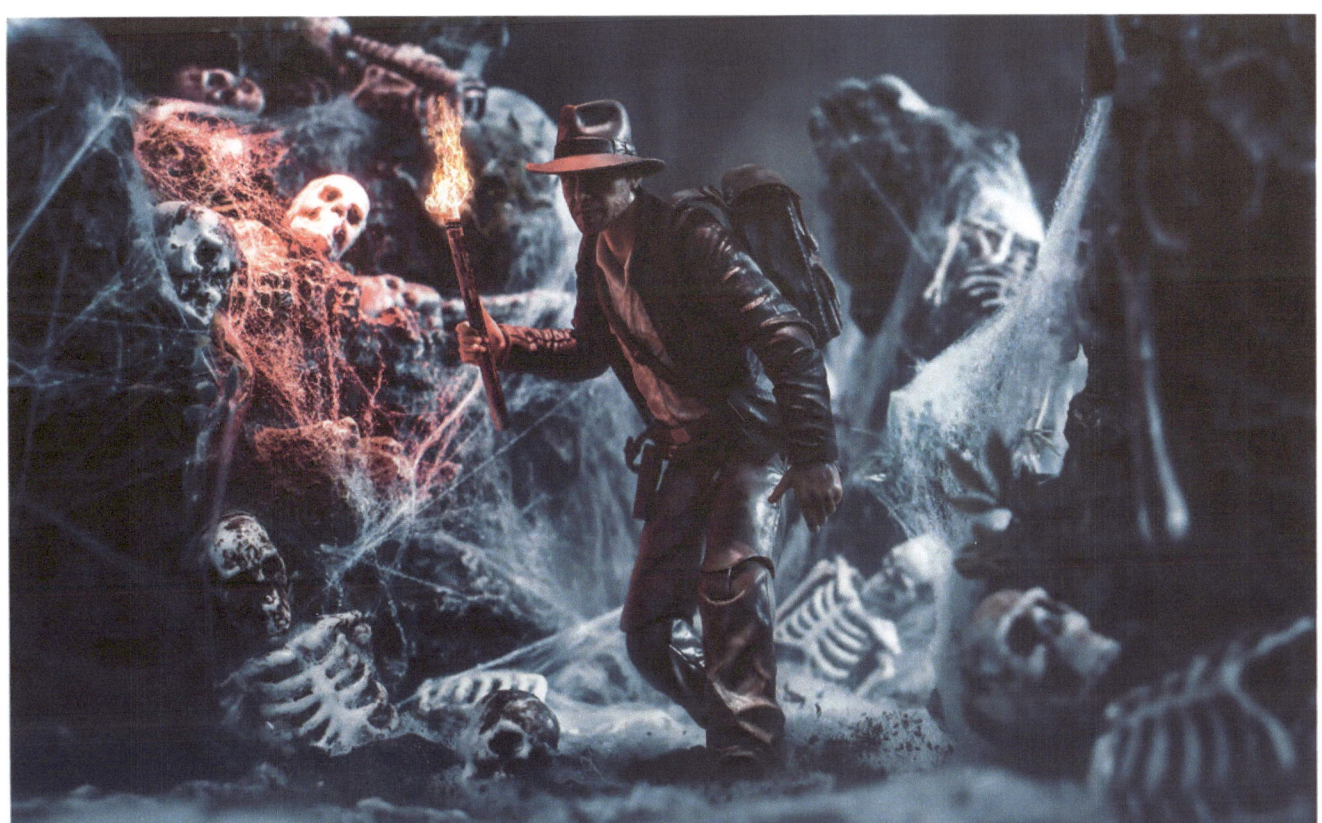

I have been an Indiana Jones fan from ever since I can remember, and 2023 gave us the amazing Indiana Jones Adventure Series line, which has allowed me to recreate the same adventures I used to act out as a kid with my figures, and has led to this, one of my all time favourite pics! - **@97_parsecs_photography**

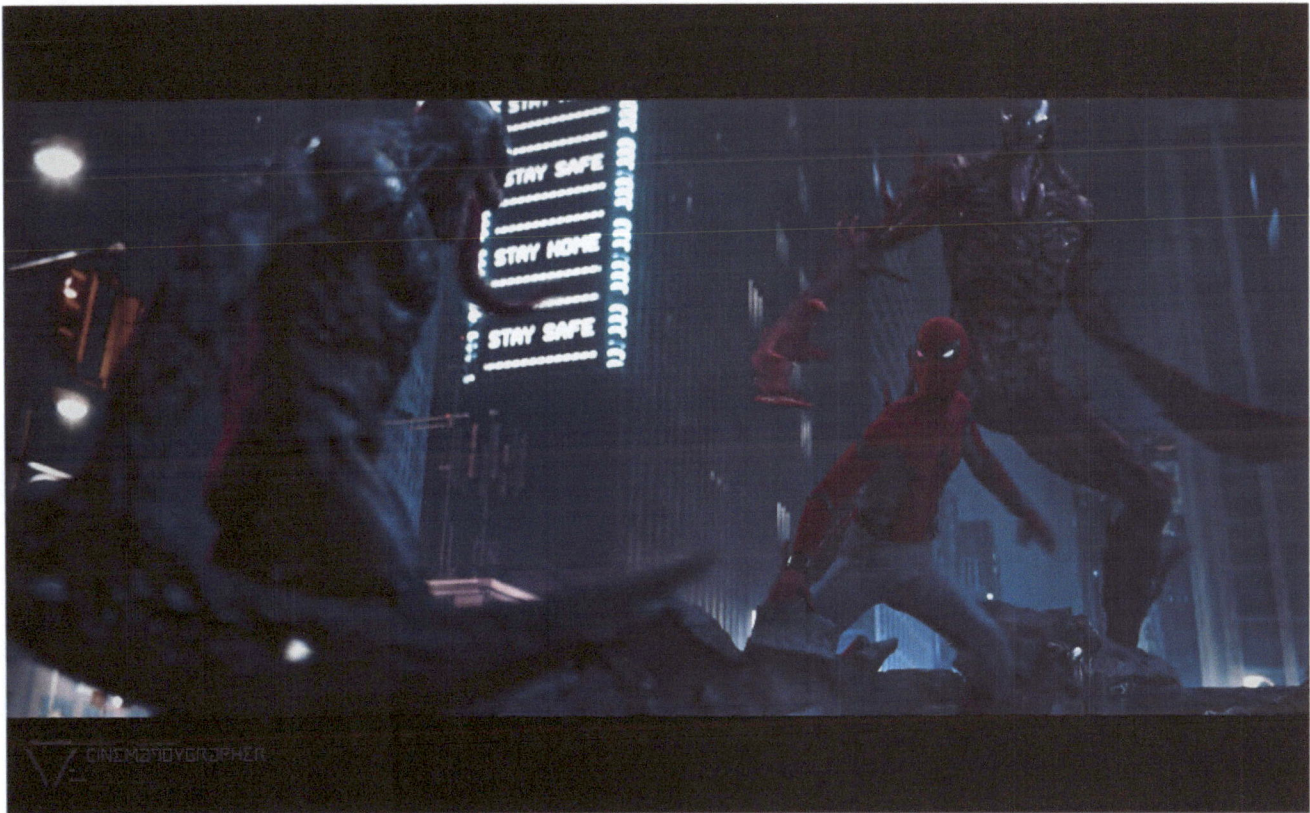

This shot is something I've always imagined in my head when I was a kid when I had the cheap plastic versions. To be able to finally create this scene in 1/6 scale made my 10 year old self really happy.
- **@_cinematoygrapher_**

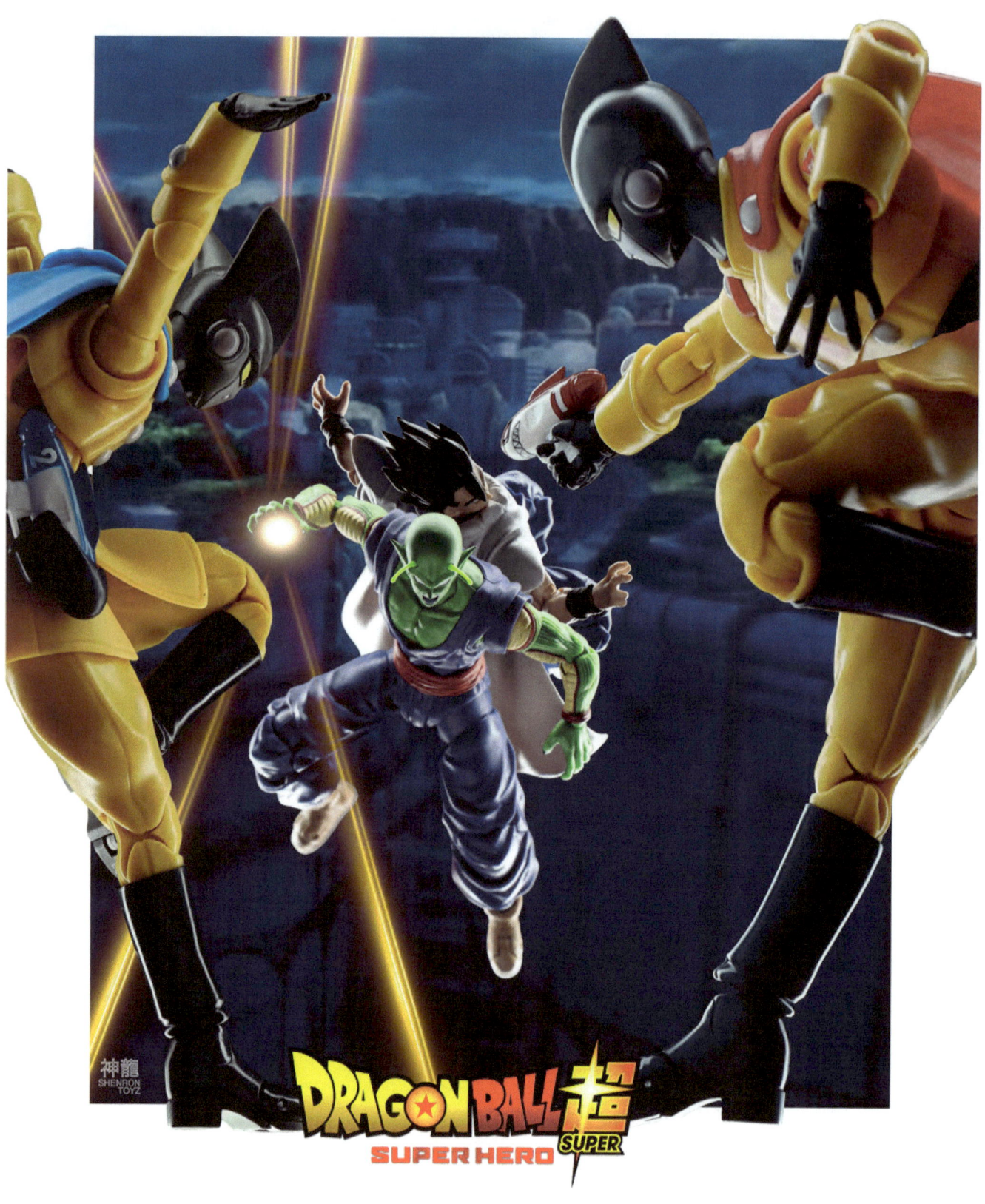

I've always been a fan of the Dragon Ball manga and anime. When I heard that a new movie would come out I was ecstatic. For me Dragon Ball is something magical that has taught me a lot of valuable lessons, being able to live the nostalgia in my adulthood is simply phenomenal. **- @Shenrontoyz**

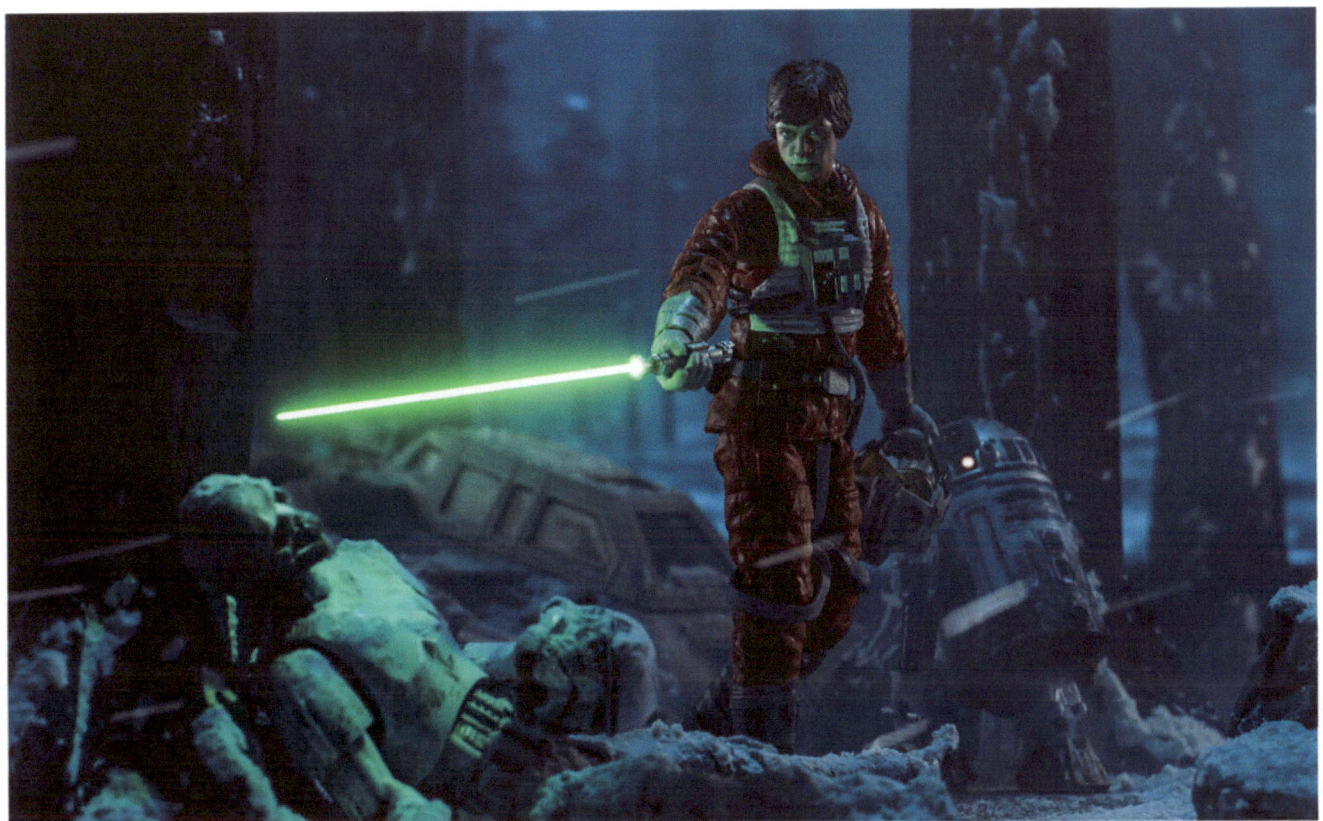

"We better keep moving, Artoo. Don't wanna end up like him." - **@press_pause_photography**

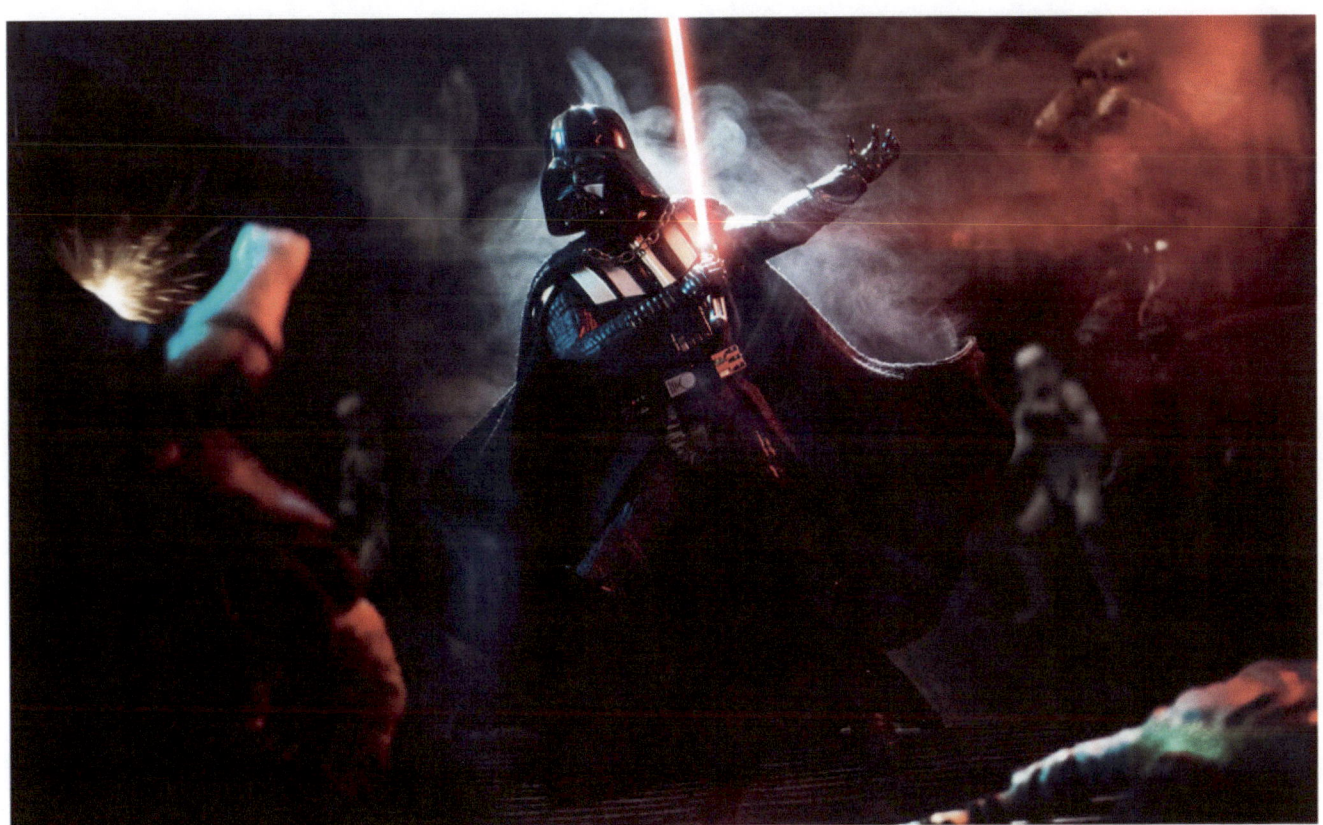

I recently got this SHFiguarts Darth Vader figure, and oh my, is it a beast! The amount of different options for hands alone give this Vader figure so many cool posing options. It really does look outstanding, and it has an imposing presence, a presence I've not felt since... - **@UmbraToyPhotos**

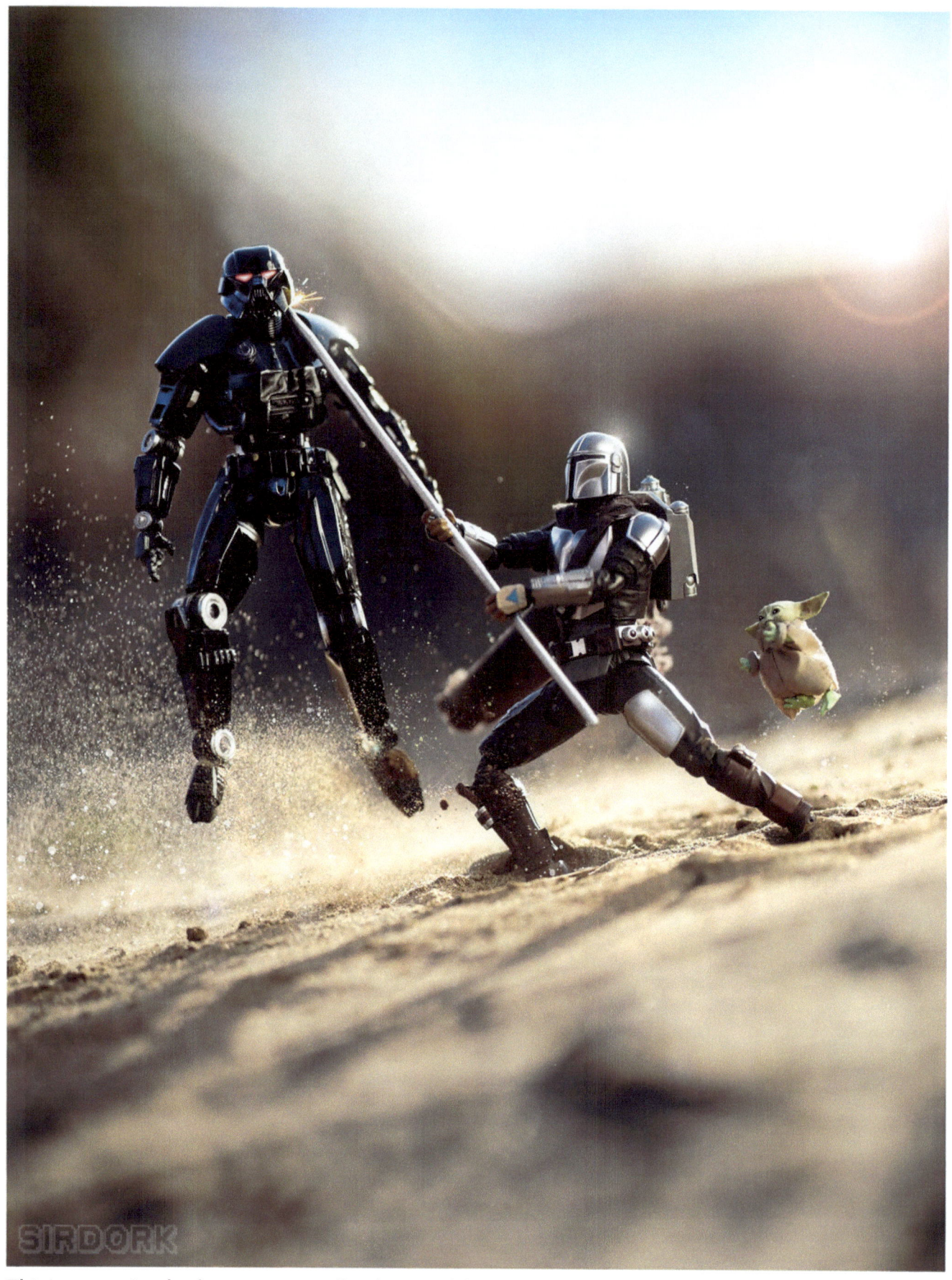

This is a very simple photo conceptually! The Mandalorian taking out a Dark Trooper in a kick-butt way using a easy custom made Beskar Spear (using a wooden skewer and silver paint). Sometimes simple ideas give more wiggle room for cool effects and visuals! - **@Sir.dork**

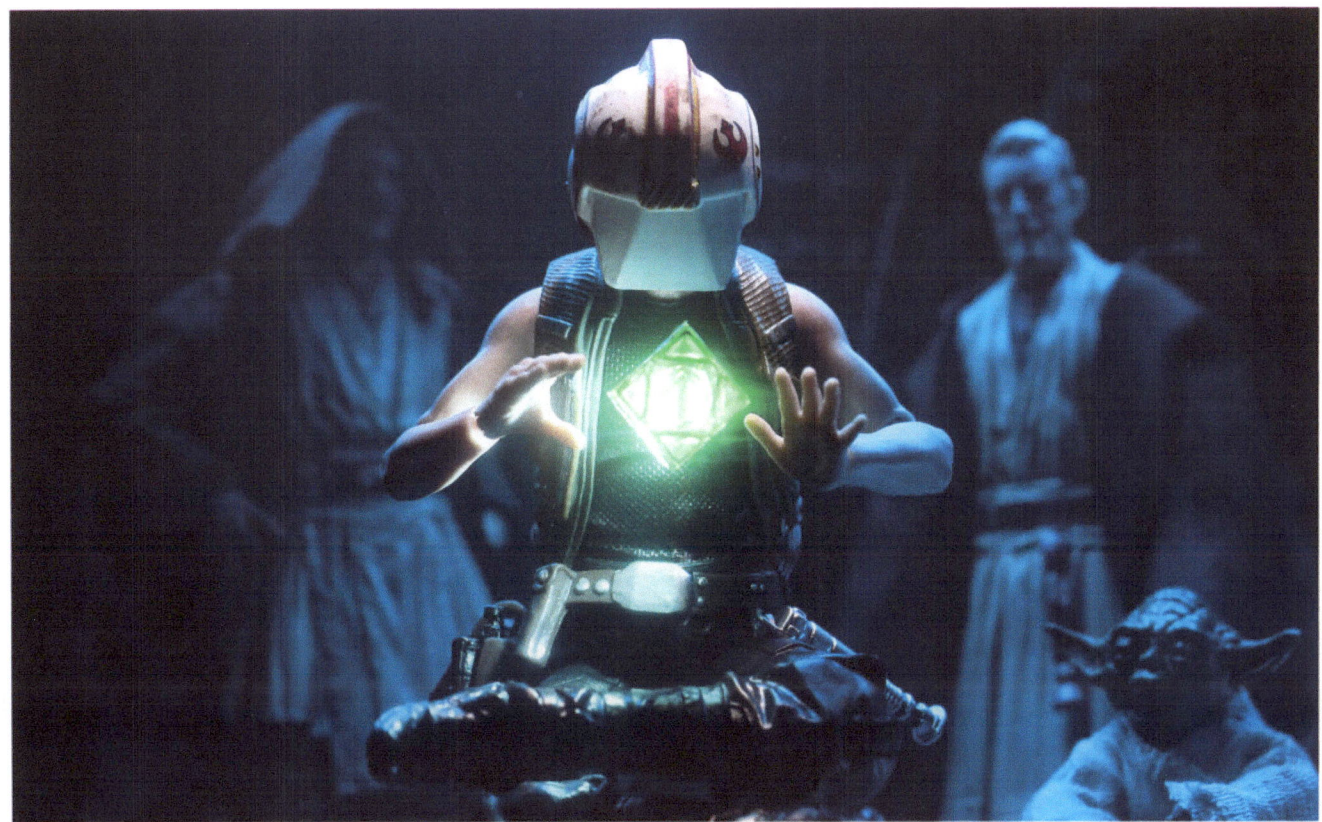

Throughout my time with toy photography, I was able to utilize all the different skills and techniques I have learned in photography to create this scene, entirely through practical, in-camera effects. It's so rewarding to capture an image exactly how you envisioned it! - **@Ripik__Tan**

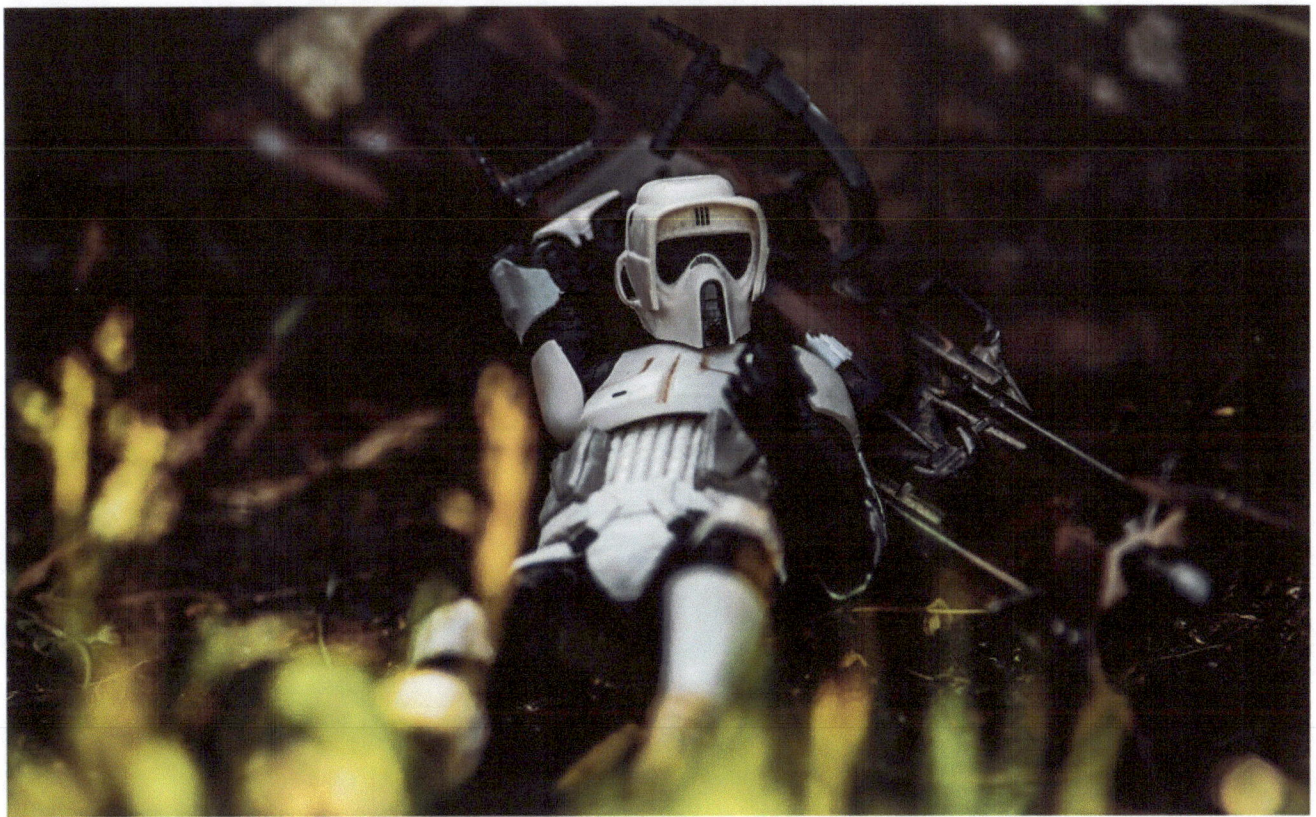

Breaktime on Endor - **@grand.moff.murdoc**

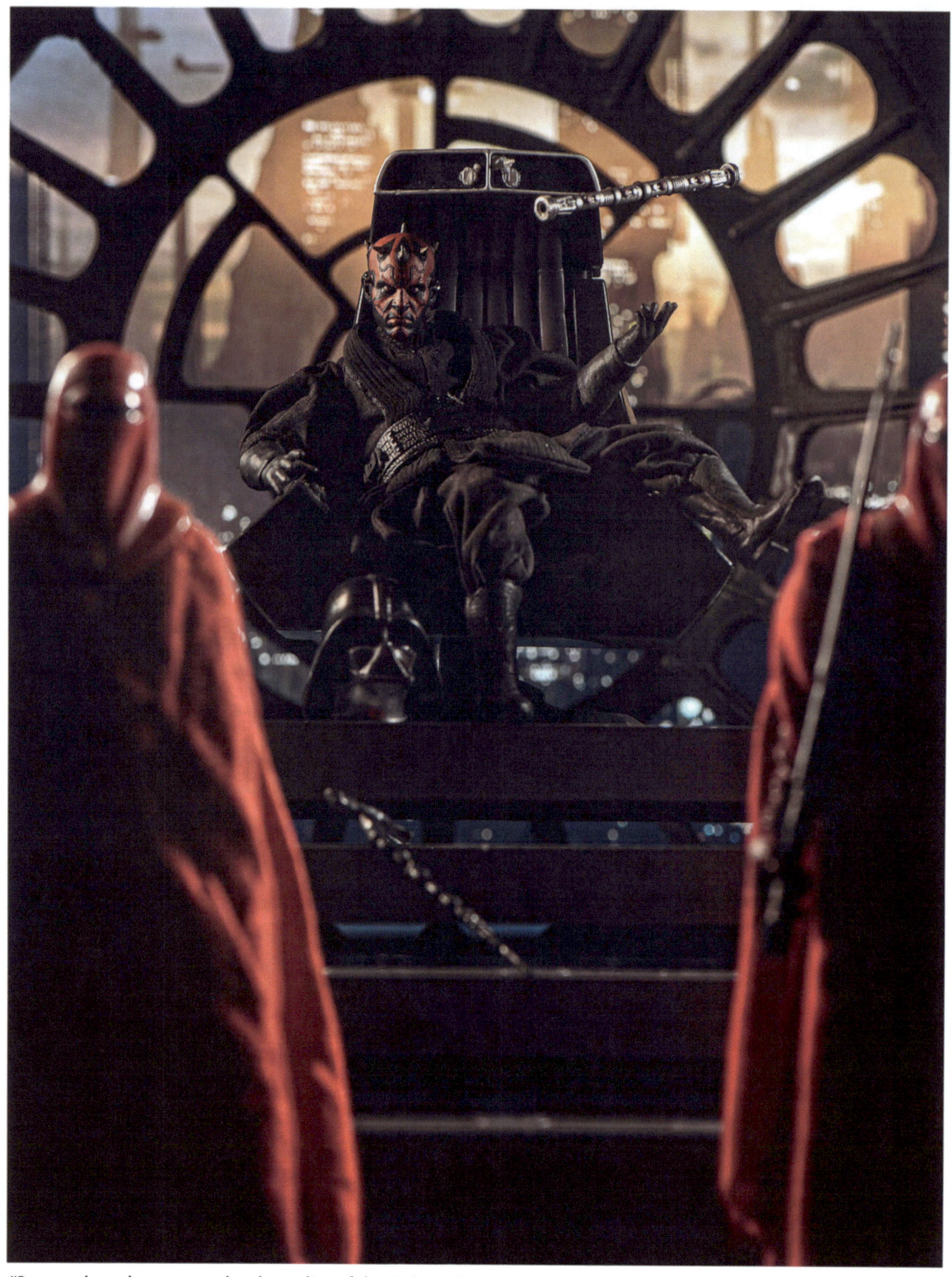

"Remember, the new and only reality of the Sith… there can only be one." - **@truupperi**

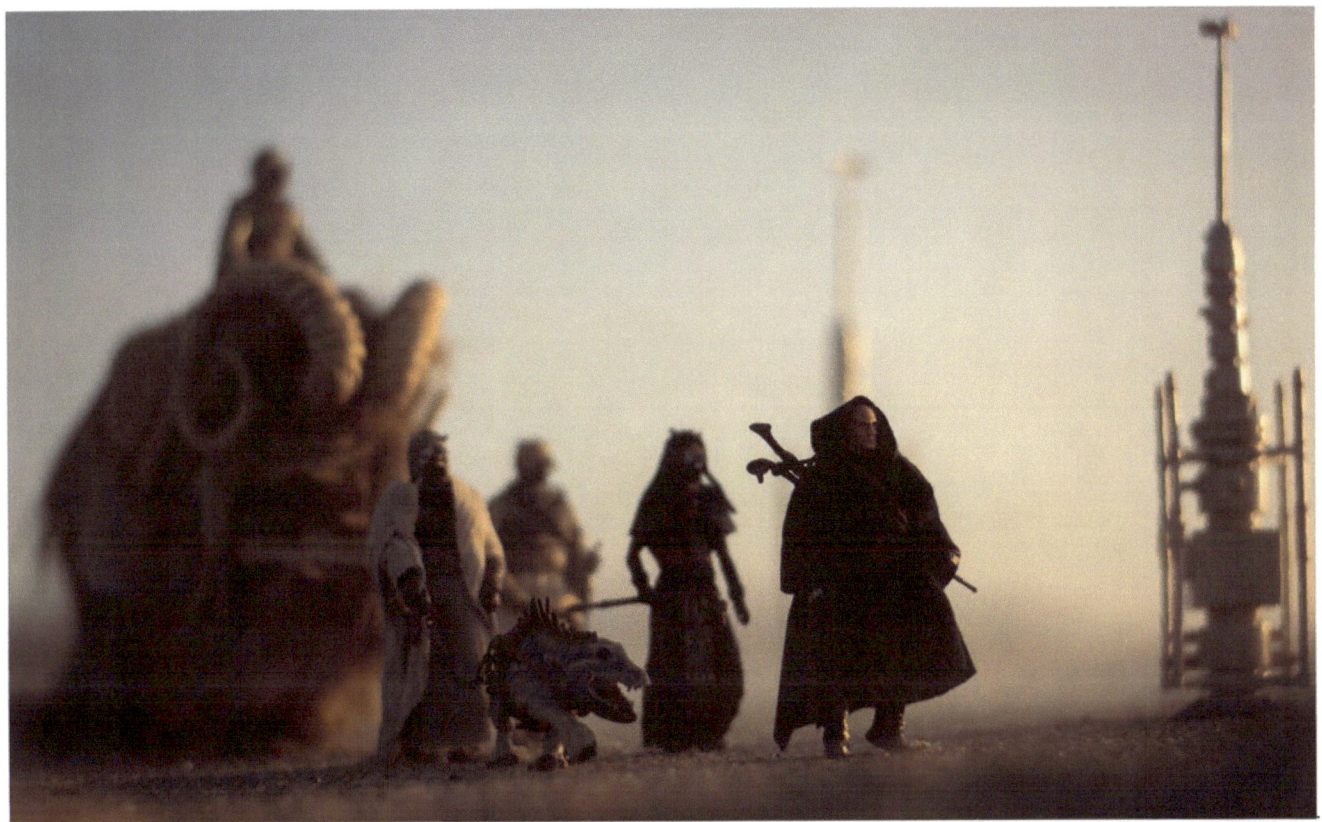

*"Leader of the Pack." - Really loved seeing Boba's totally immersion into Tusken life. I wanted to portray how he became one of them and their acceptance of him into the 'family. - @**Chezpics66***

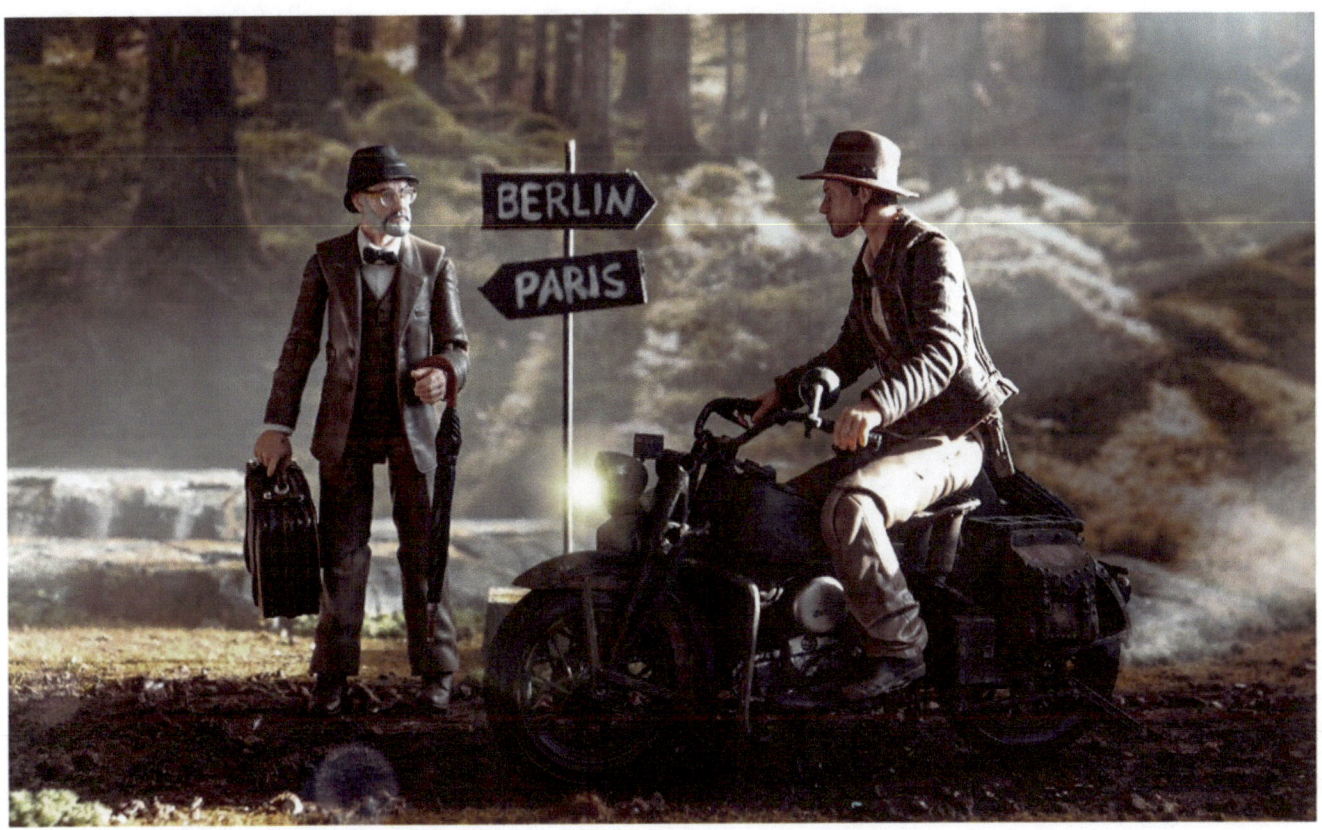

*Dr. Henry Jones: "We have to go to Berlin, Junior." - @**chewie_the_pooh***

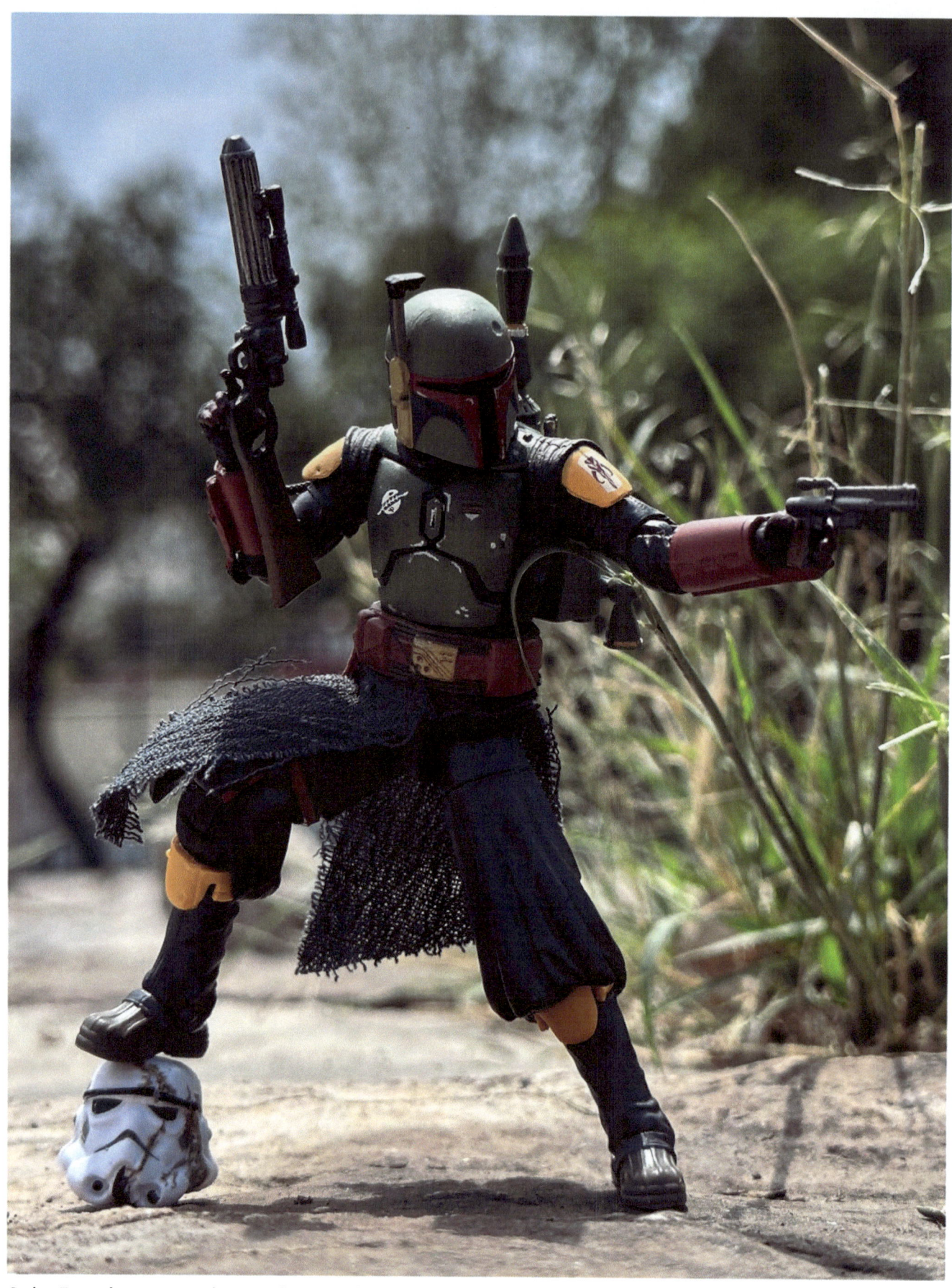

Boba Fett, the greatest bounty hunter of the entire galaxy! I'm showing how's good the articulation of this 3.75 figure. An outdoor pic, our friend is the sun, Boba is holding his 2 blasters stepping on a damaged stormtrooper helmet. - **@abs_collectibles.sw**

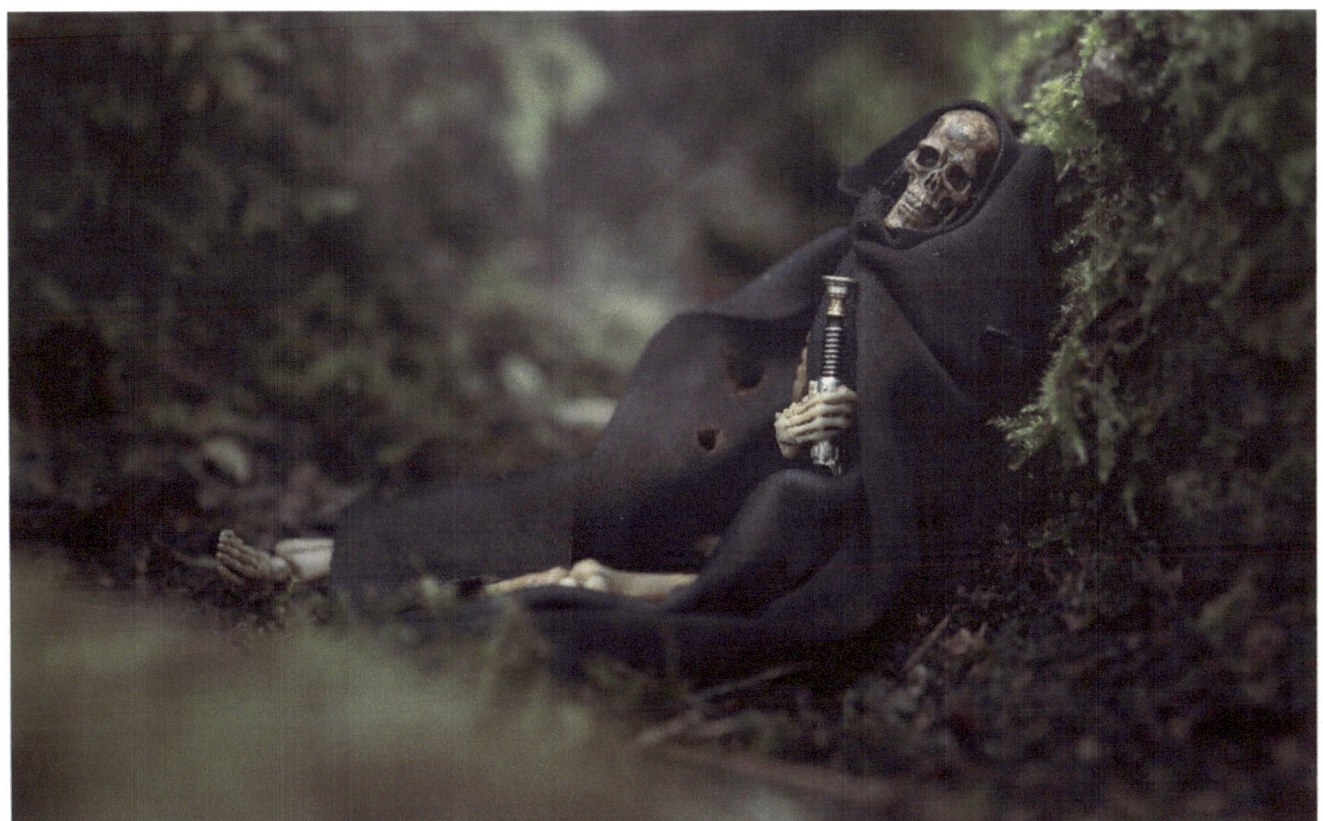

Death is a natural part of life. Rejoice for those around you who transform into the Force. Mourn them do not. Miss them do not. Attachment leads to jealously. The shadow of greed, that is. - **@frame_the_toys**

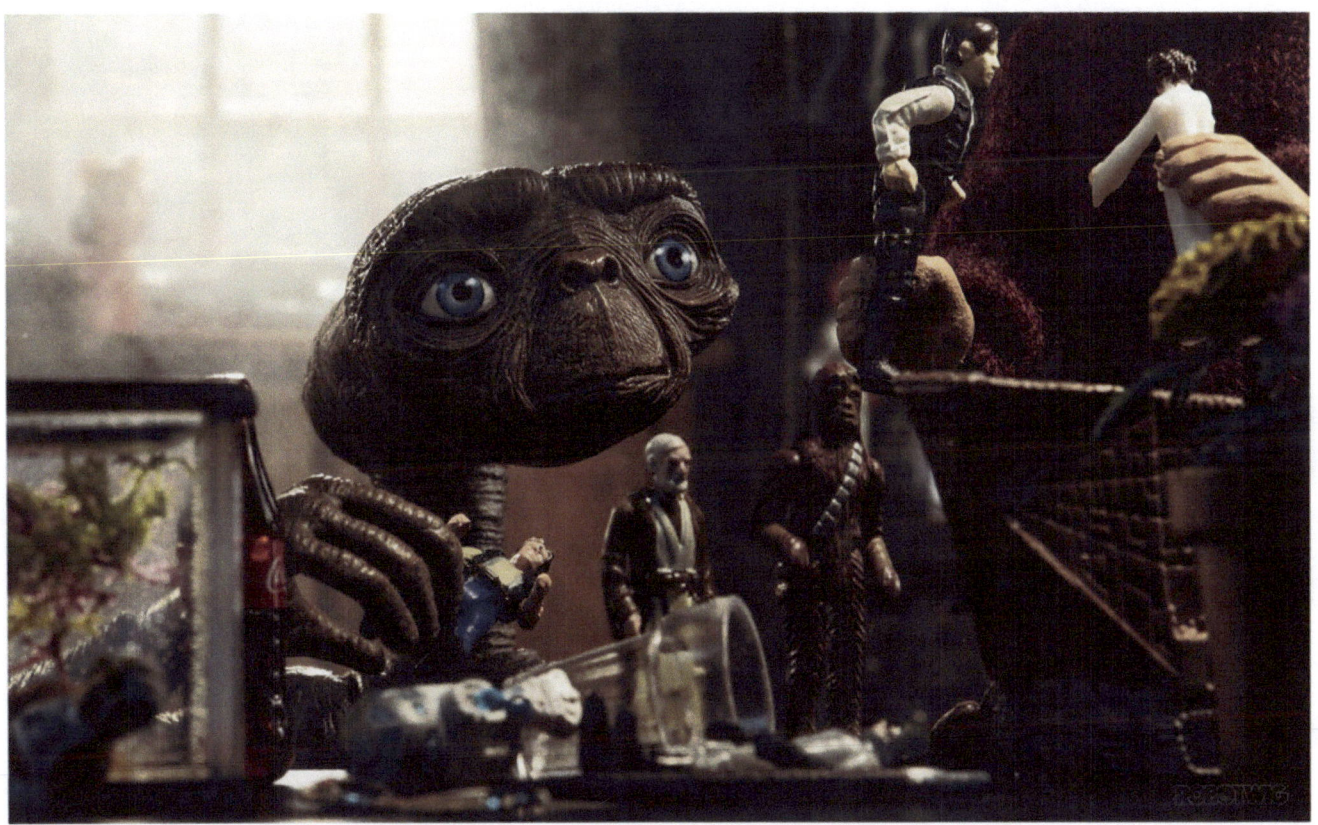

"Coke. You see, we drink it. It's a, it's a drink. You know, food. These are toys, these are little men…" - I'm a big fan of E.T. and really wanted to capture the quiet moment with Elliot showing E.T. around his room. All my photos are shot practically so everything you see is really there. - **@RobotWig**

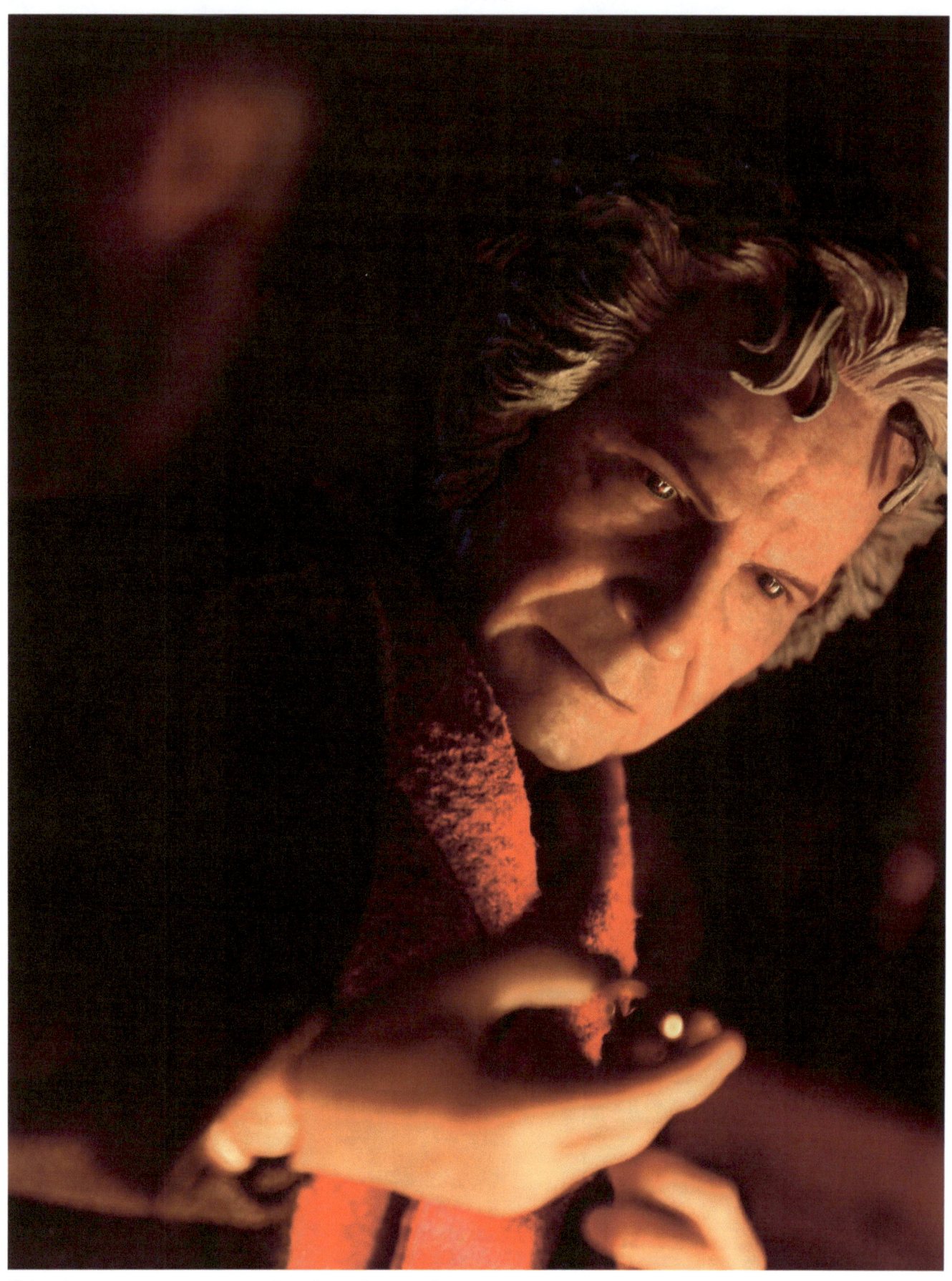

"It's mine…my own…my precious." - **@ab_toypics**

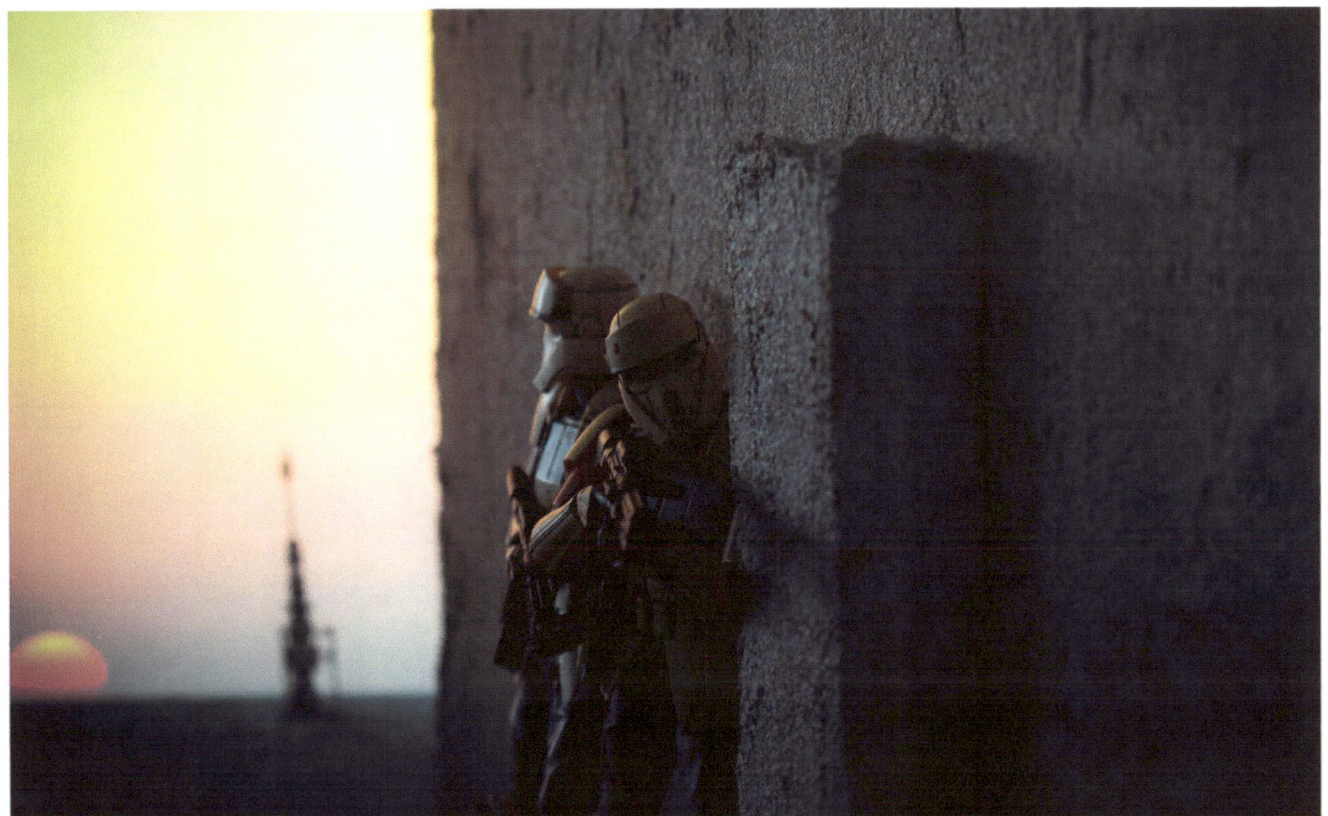

Shootout at sundown - For this image, I've attempted to blend a digital background with the figures and scratch made building. - @CBPrints3D

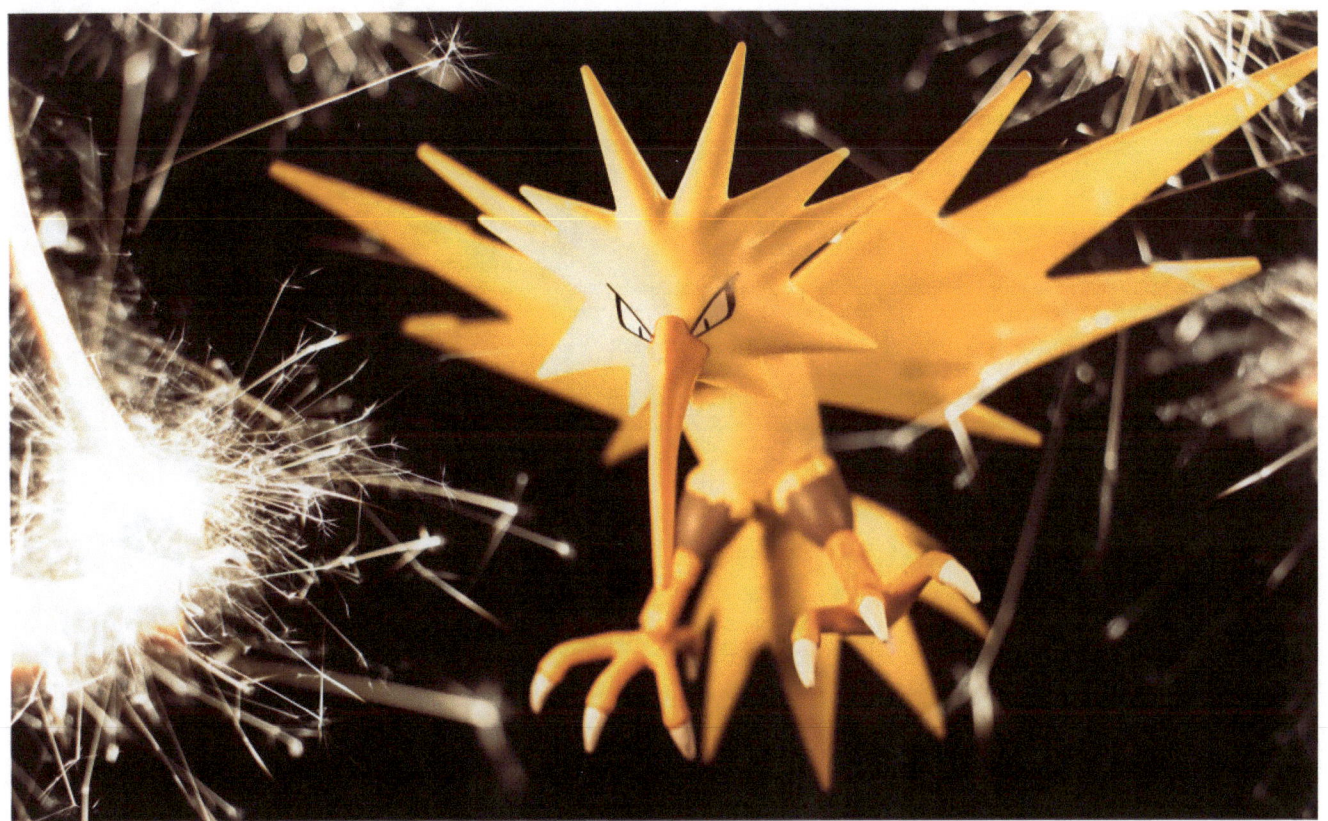

Thunderwave - @_ianparra

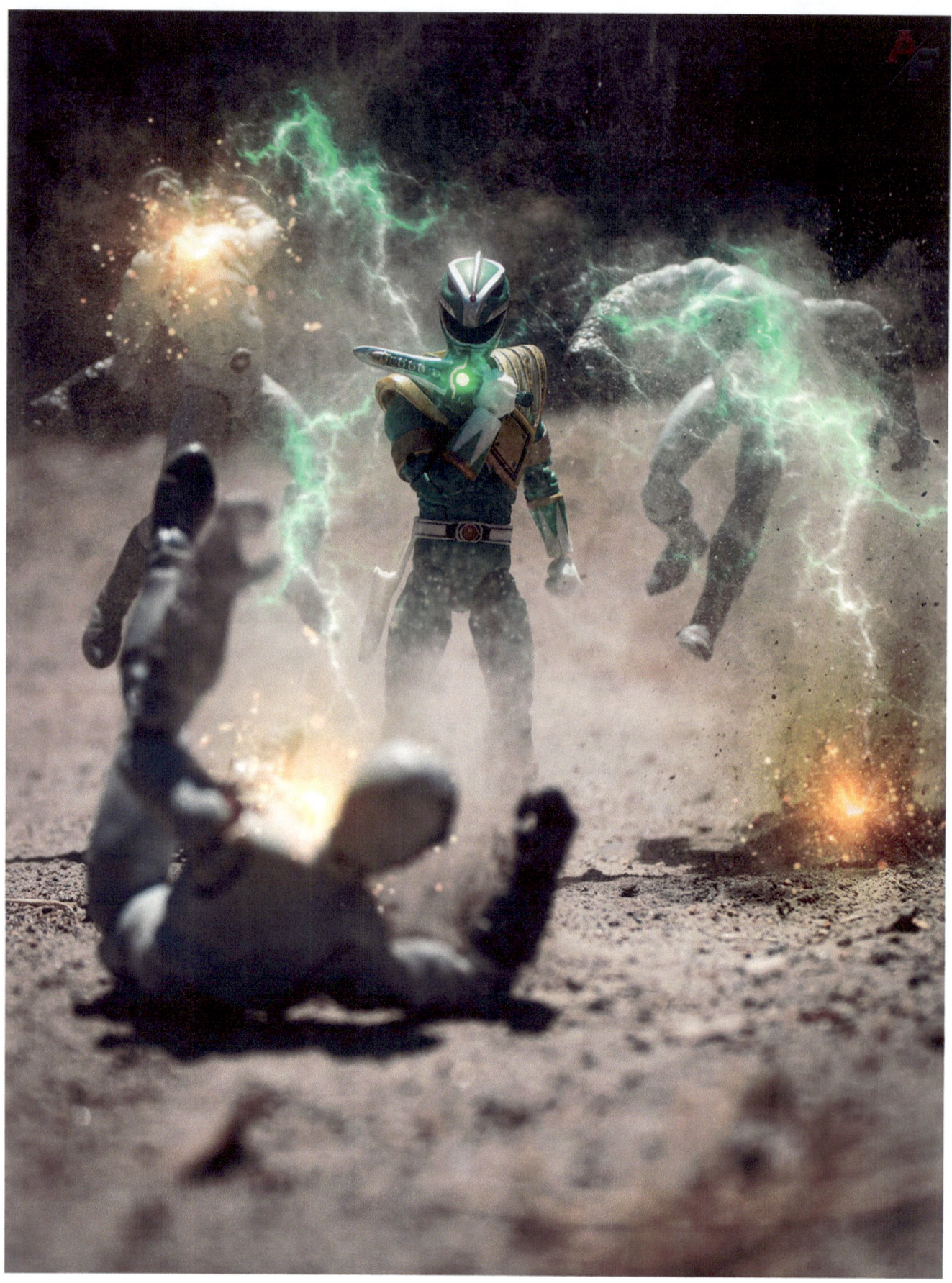

Im a big Power Rangers fan and a huge fan of the Green Ranger, with the passing of the actor I was really inspired to do something really cool and to represent the awesomeness of the Green Ranger! If you're a 90's kid this is dedicated to you because I know we all loved Tommy Oliver! RIP JDF - @actionfiguresnapz

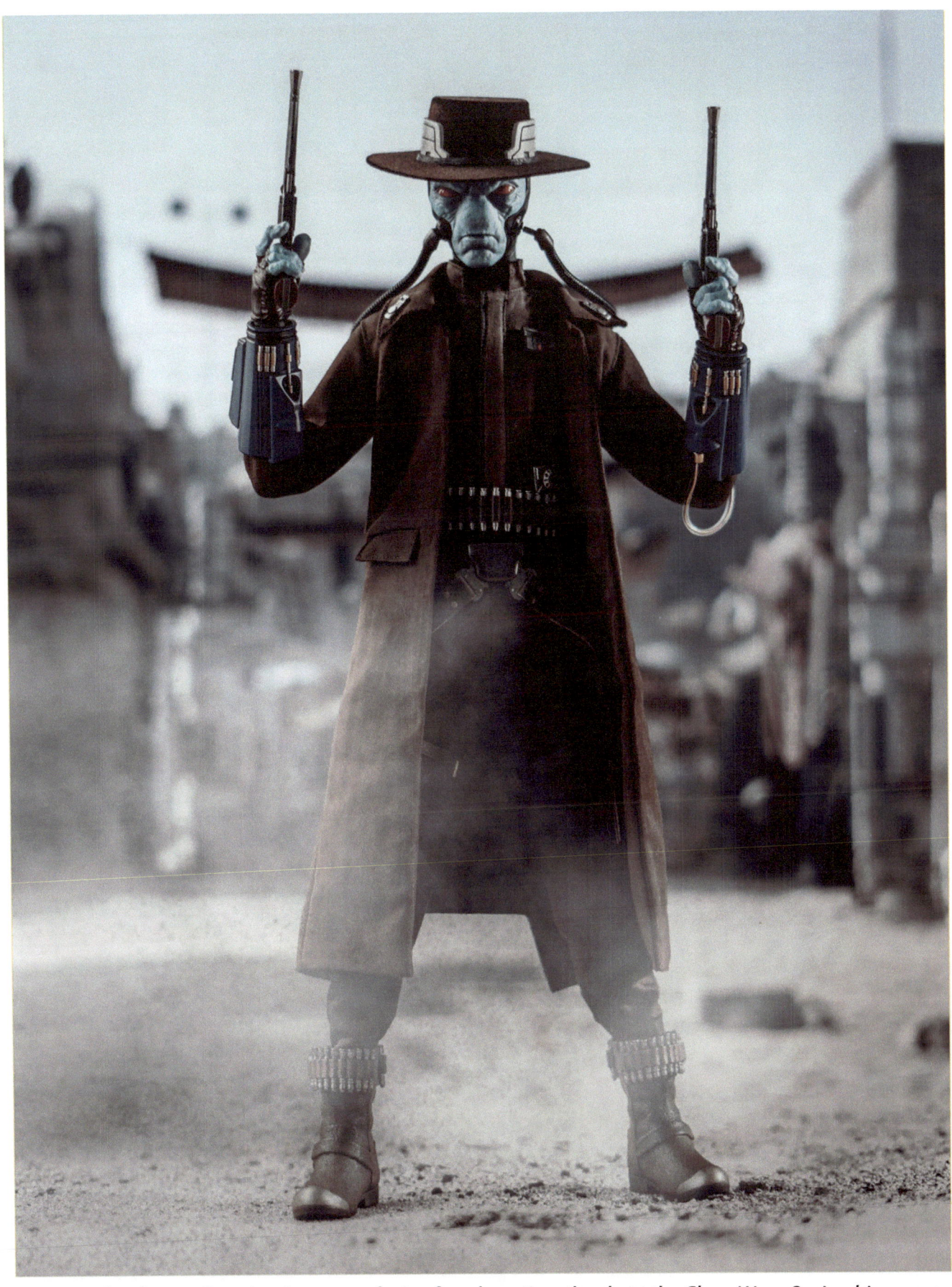

Cad Bane has been a favorite character of mine for a long time thanks to the Clone Wars. Seeing him come to life in The Book Of Boba was awesome and to have a mini version of him in hand is insane!
- **@mythosboba**

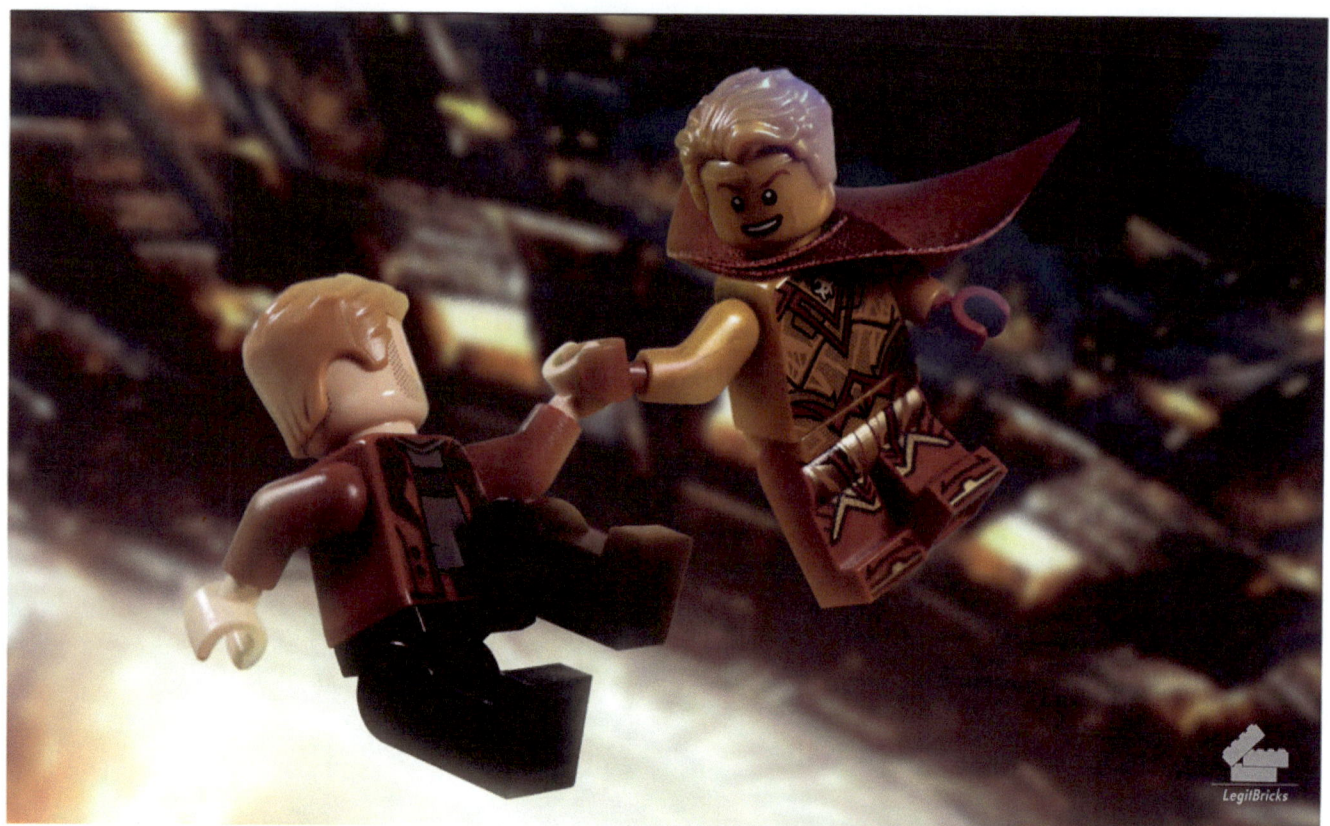

This is a parody scene where Adam Warlock saves Star-Lord's life in GOTG Vol.3. Parodying the mural "Creation of Adam" in the film felt so creative, so it inspired me to re-create the scene with LEGO.
*- @legitbricks_*

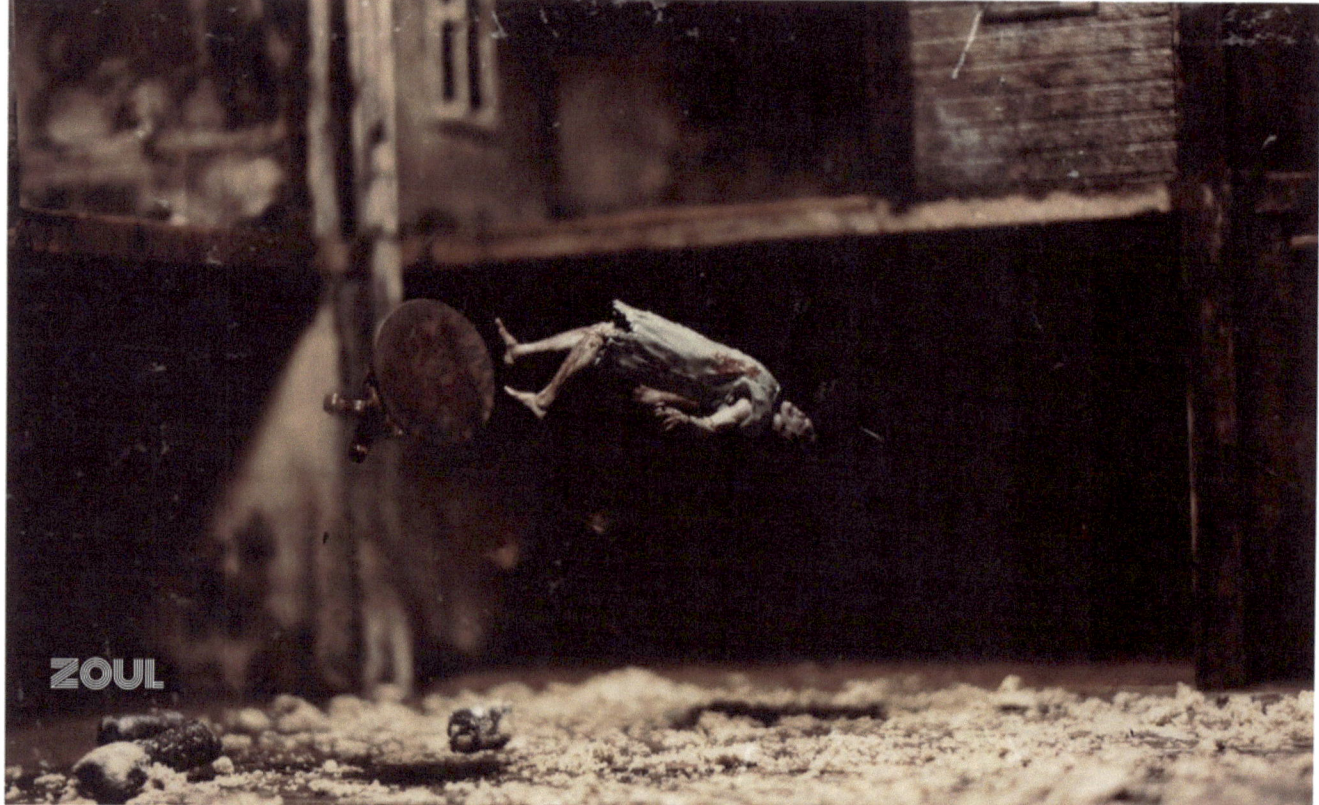

Levitation - this shot I got the idea from a horror movie in the 90s... I remember this scene.... and it freaked me out....still until today..... - @ZoulHajiz

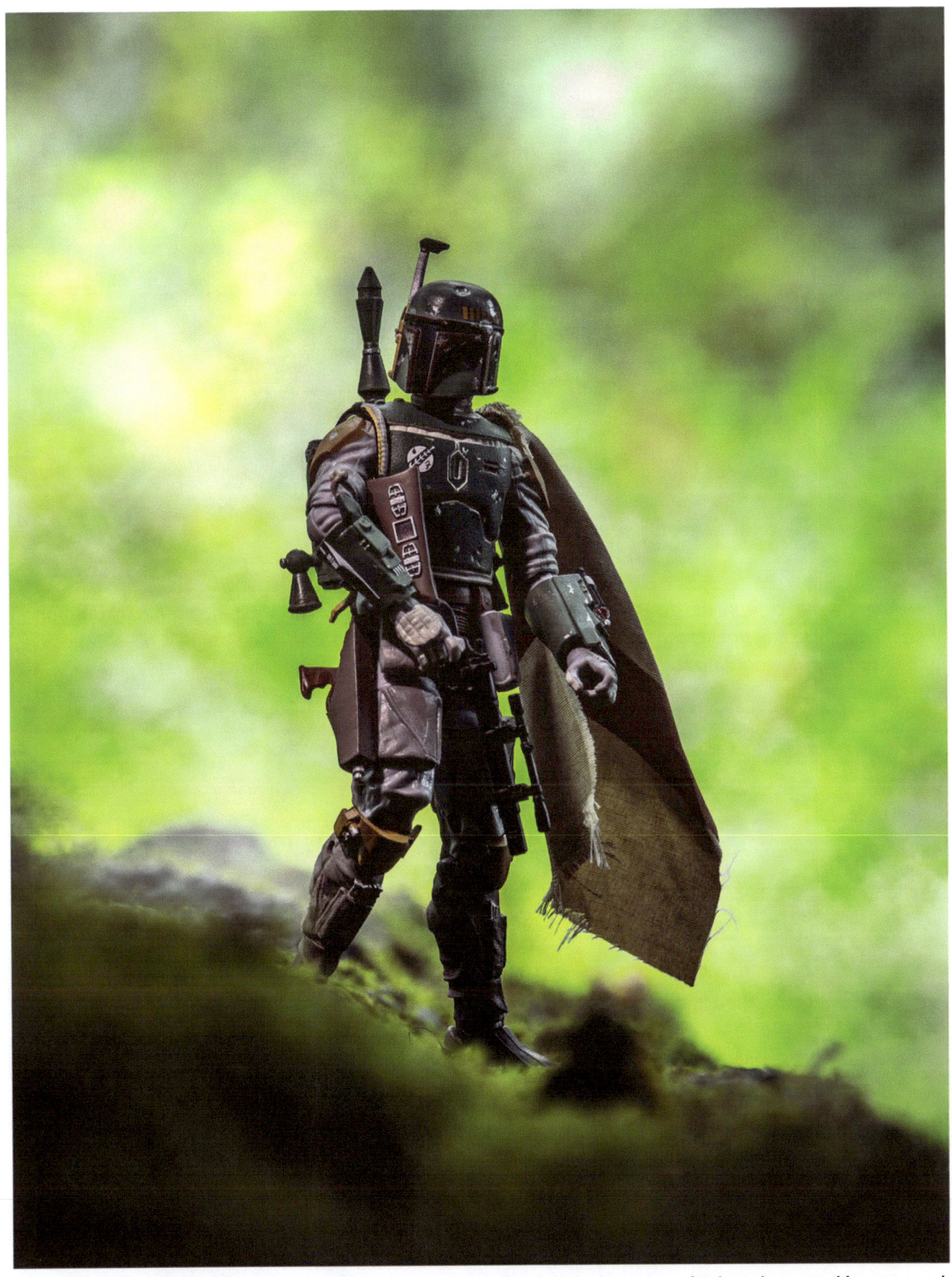

Ever since I was a kid watching Star Wars, I was obsessed with Boba Fett. Just thinking how cool he was and mysterious, getting his figure was a big thing for me and this shot is one of my favourites so far!
- **@actiontoyphotography**

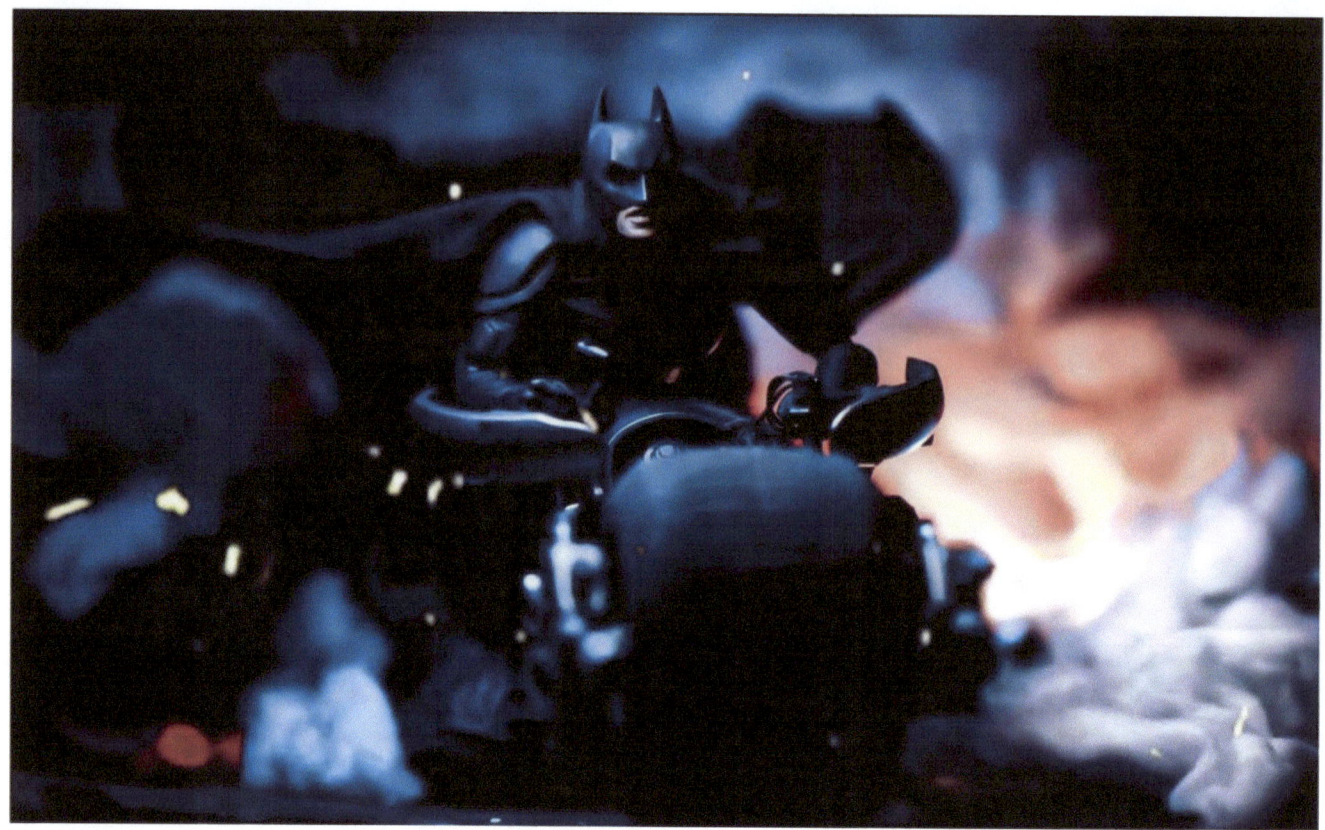

I really wanted to capture the dynamic of the explosive launch of the Bat-Pod and the posture of Batman with his cape gusting out behind, racing to capture the Joker . Great face sculpts by Mafex, delicate posing and lots of cotton wool with coloured lights gave the desired effect. **- @thebrninv**

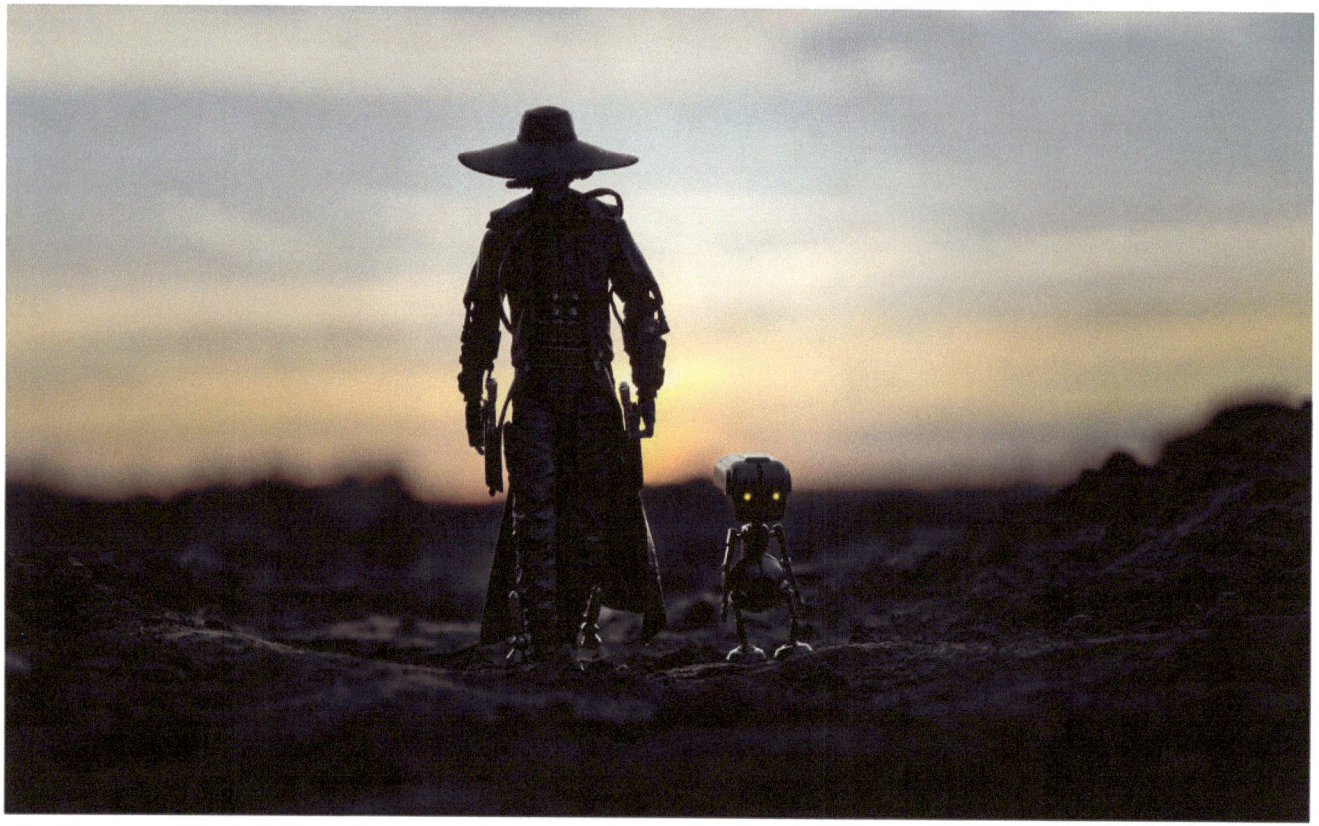

Cad Bane and Todo 360 - **@Geo_76_photography**

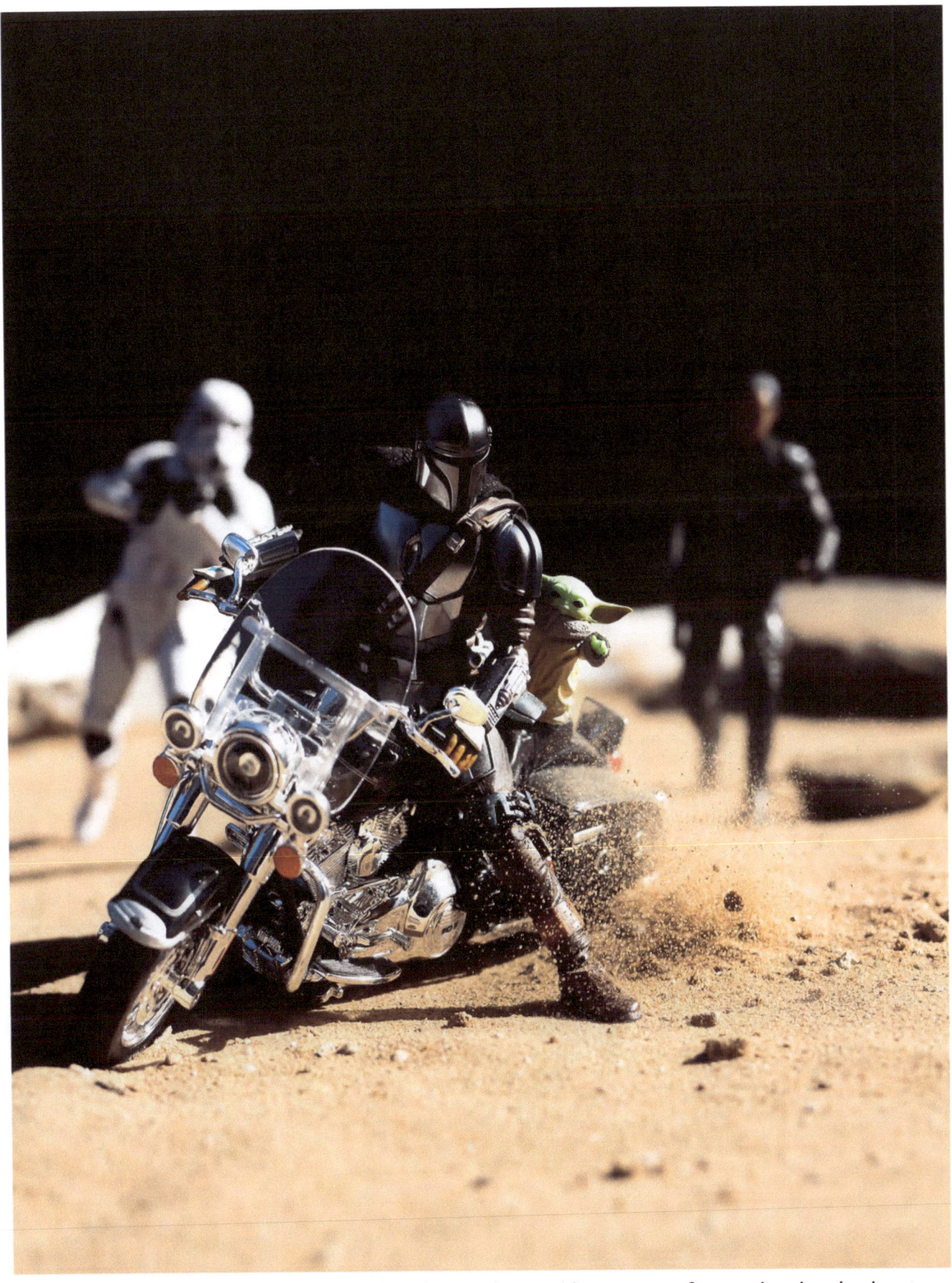

*Hold on, Kid! - I enjoy creating practical effects for my photos. I blew up some fine sand and took advantage of the morning sunshine. - **@andrea_toyphotography***

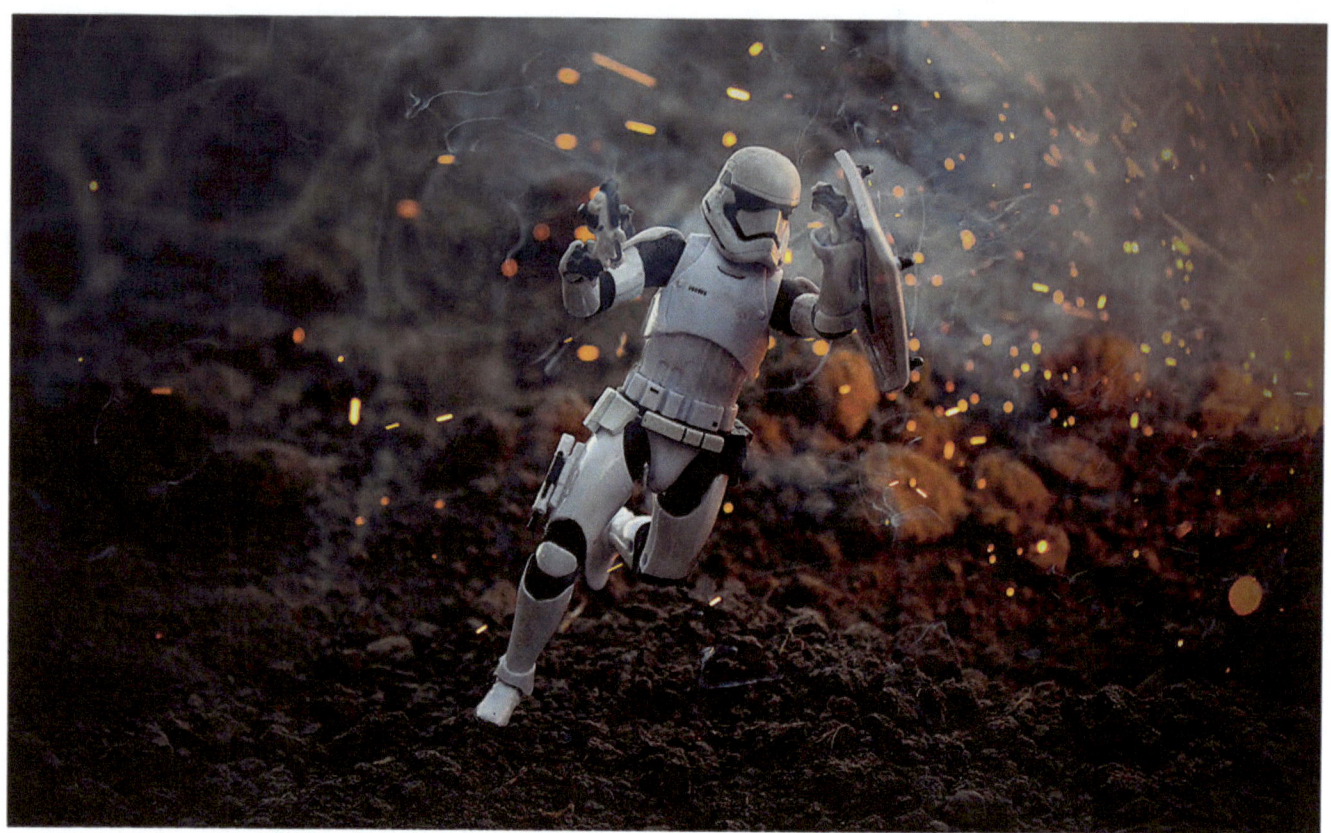

Born in the Storm - **@Dewbacked**

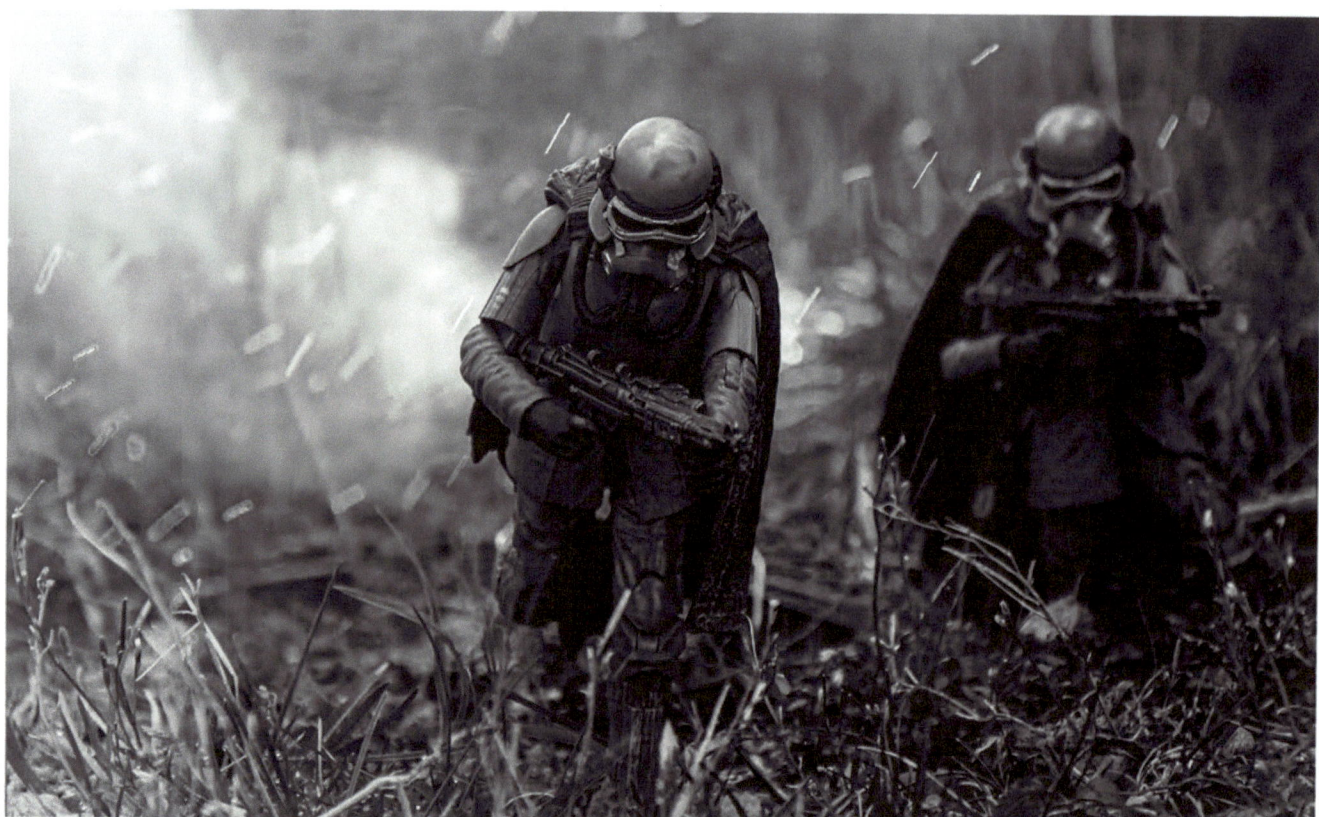

My inspiration came from watching old war movies. The image is titled - Brothers in Arms
- **@alan.laighleis**

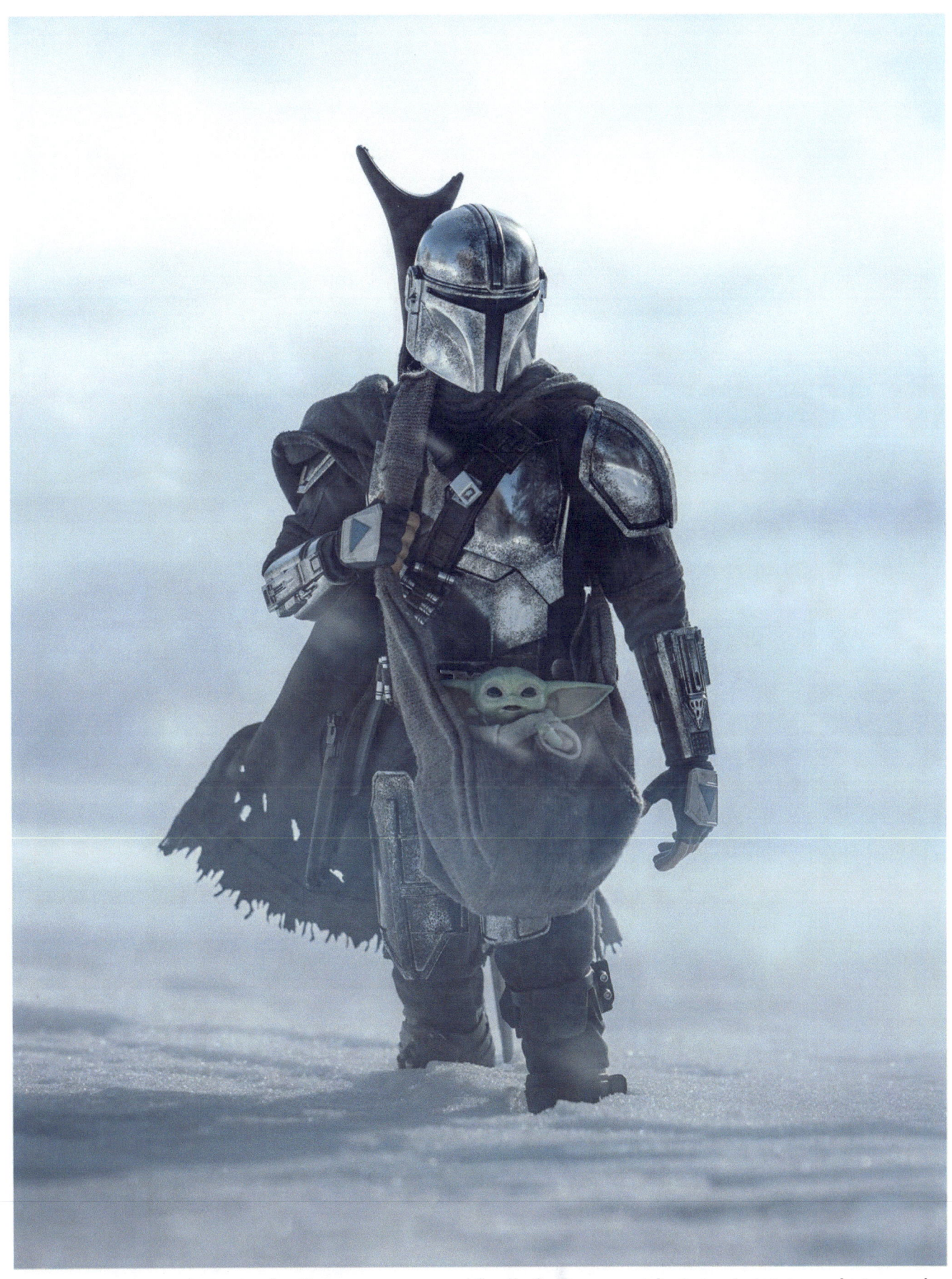

Being an amateur photographer for many years and finally finding my niche in toy/miniature photography has been such a great ride. I'm having so much fun creating. Nearly very day I wake up thinking of what photo to make next. - @jessefeyereisen

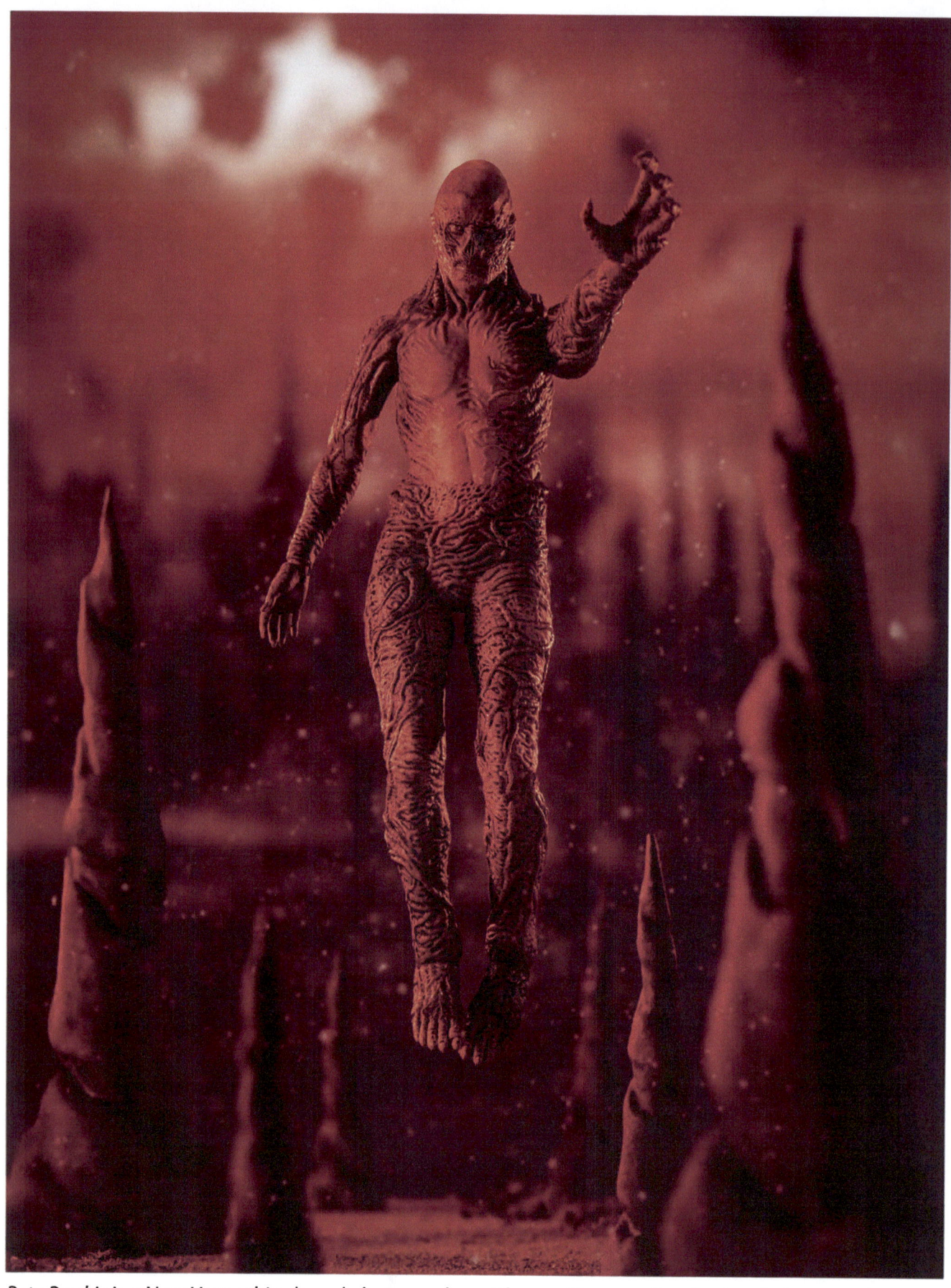

*Pete Ruokis is a New Hampshire-based photographer with over 12 years of professional photography experience. In 2020, during quarantine, Pete began to focus his work on Lego and toy photography, bringing his two biggest passions together into one artistic medium. - **@pete_ruokis_photography***

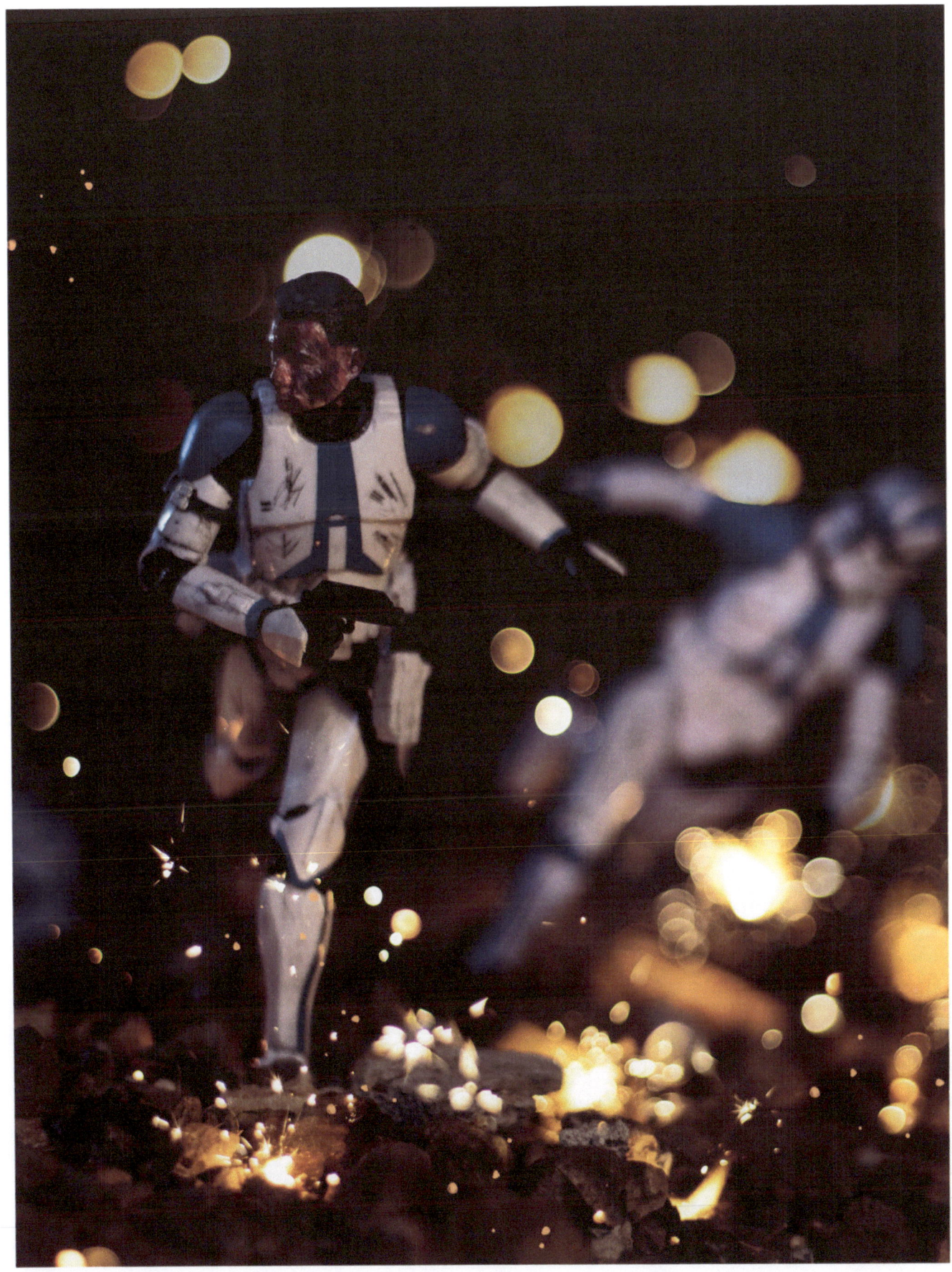

*I call this shot "The Scars Of War" because even if our character survives this battle he will still carry the scars for eternity - @**aussieactionfigs***

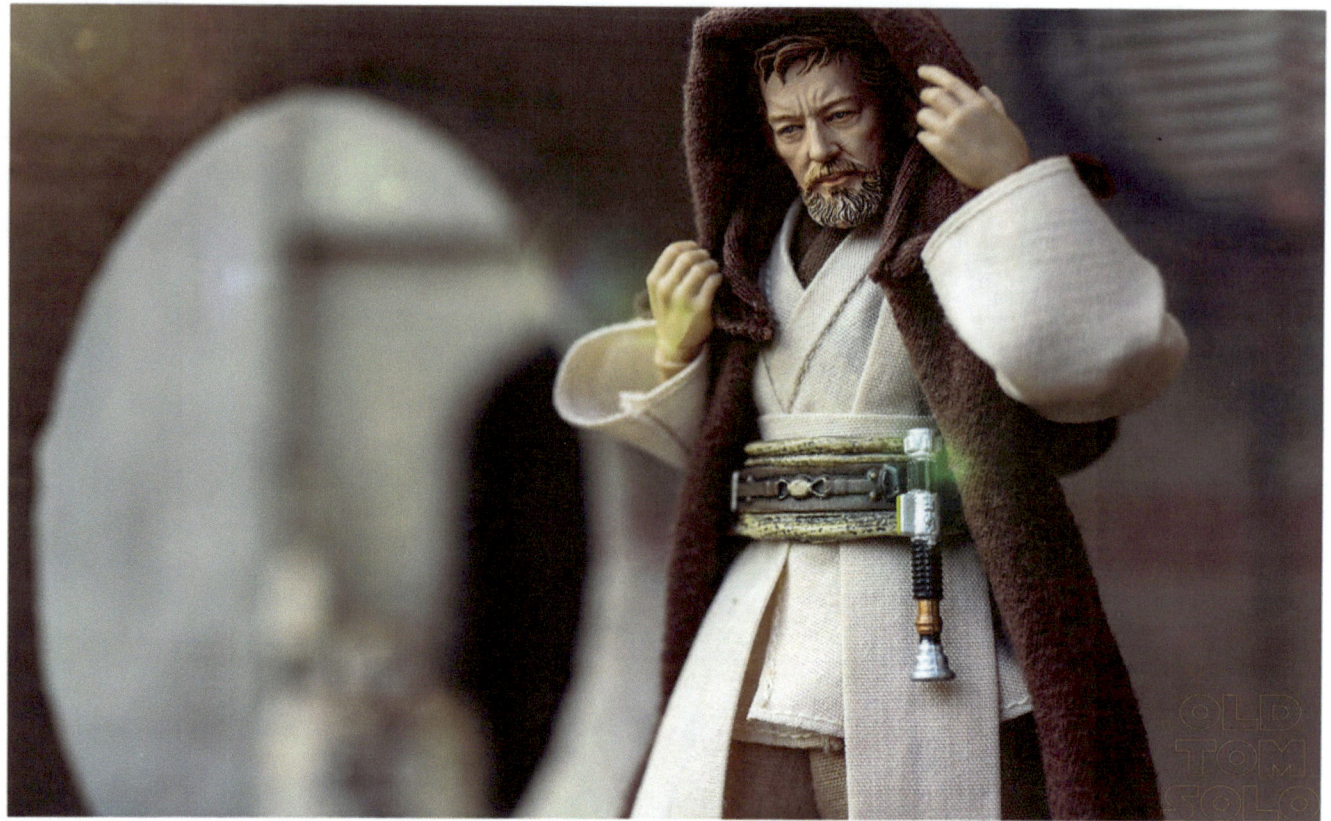

The toy photography community can be viewed very much as a niche hobby, but also as a community. A community I find to be filled with inspirational artists, and friends. It is here I prefer to spend my free time, what little of it I can find. - **@old.tom.solo**

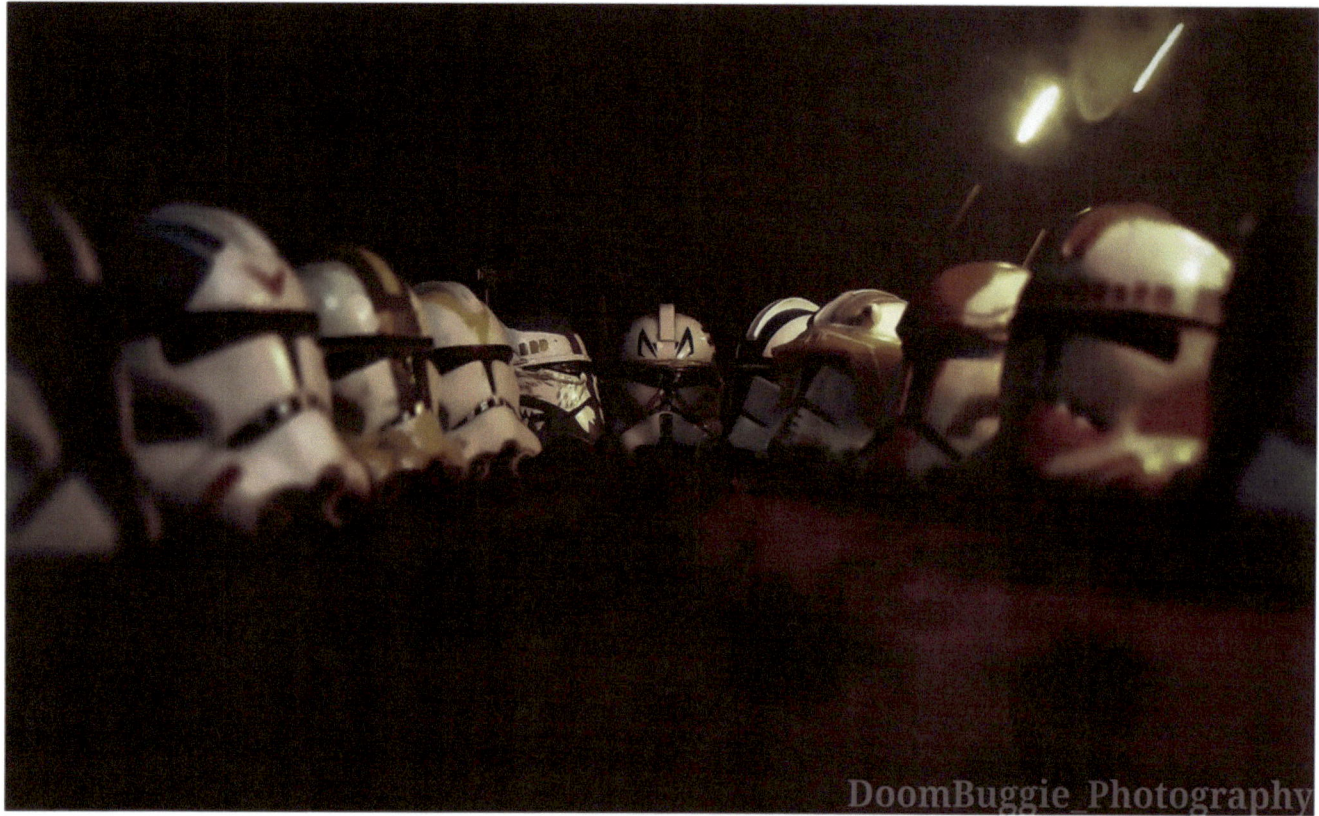

This was inspired by the emotional Clone Wars Season 7 trailer. I accidentally set the box I was using on fire . . . It took a while, but I think I captured the scene and the emotion it conveyed.
- **@Doombuggie_Photography**

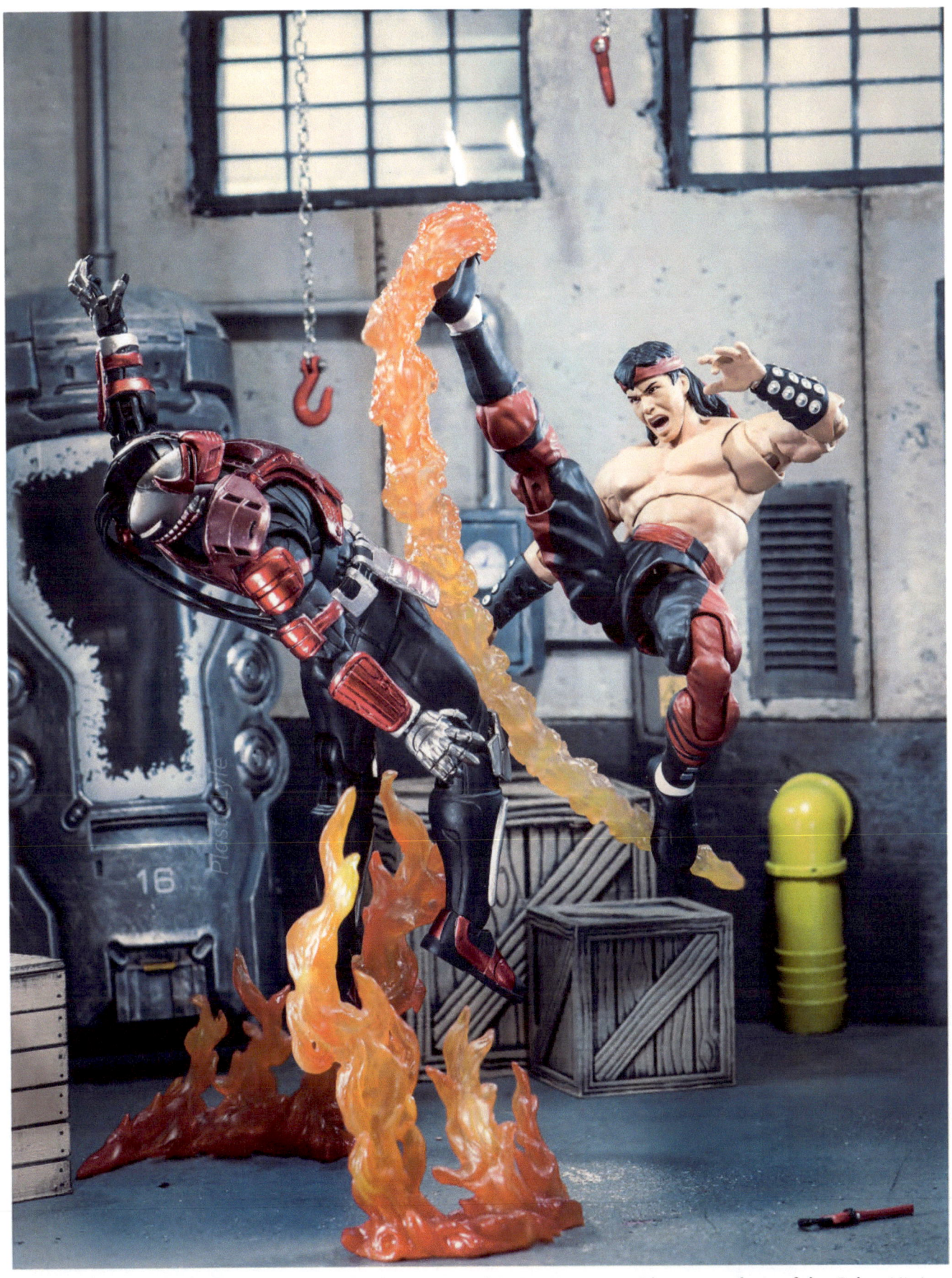

"They are physically skilled, but mentally, they are weak." - Liu Kang provides an analysis of the Cyber Ninjas
- @plastic.lyfe

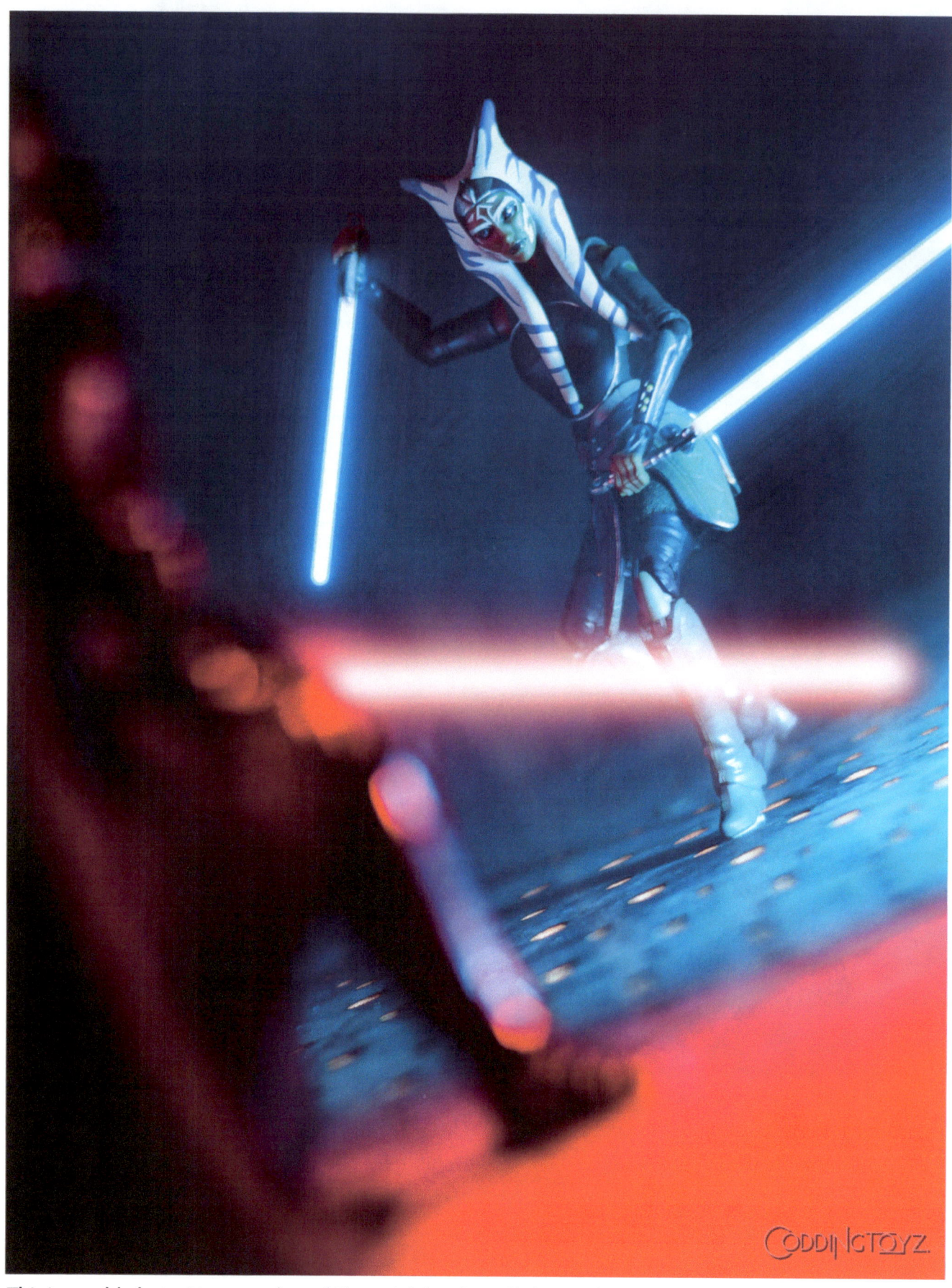

This is an old photo, I improved my skills and did technically better shots since this one but it's still one of my favorites! I'm very happy that it's featured in this book. - **@Coddingtoyz**

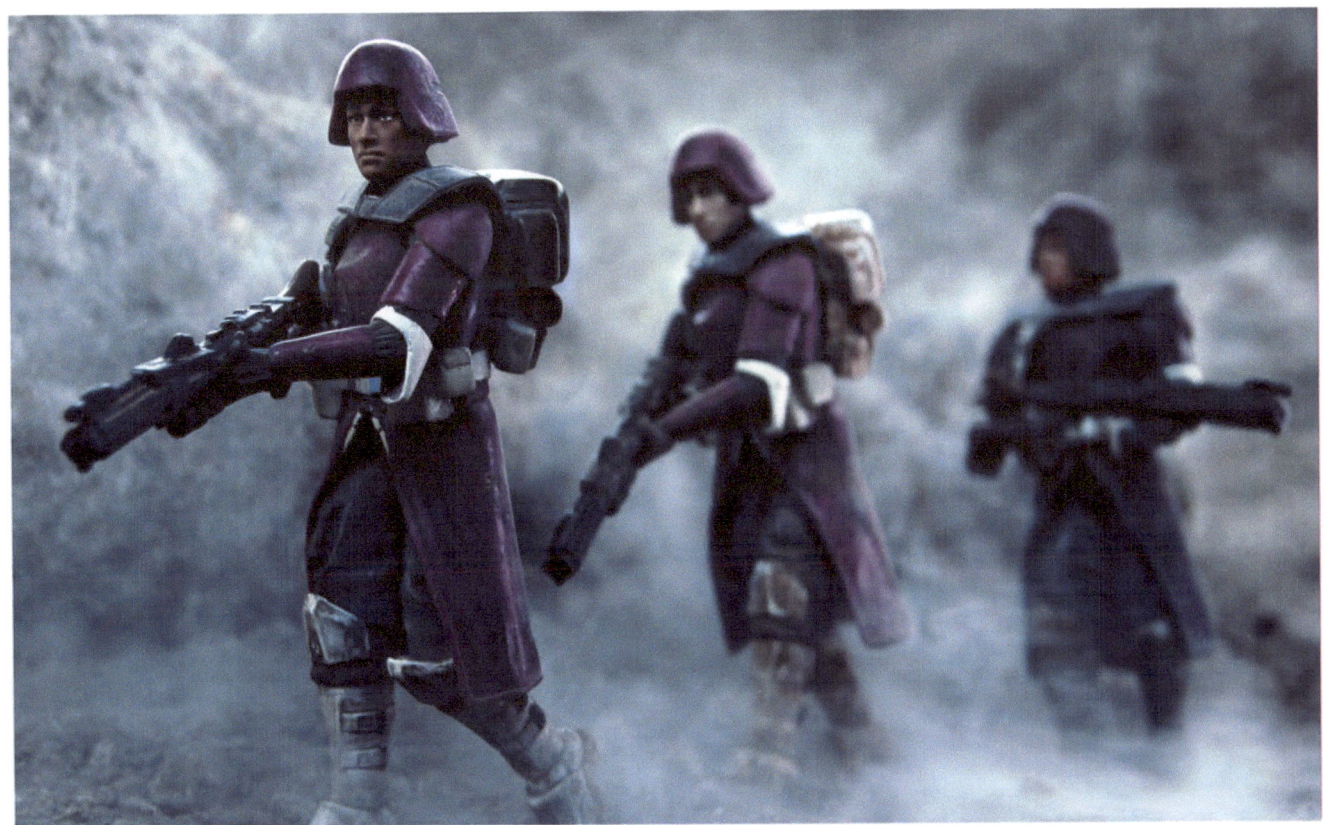

Galactic Correspondents - Bringing you news from all the fronts of the Galaxy
- @Galactic_Correspondents

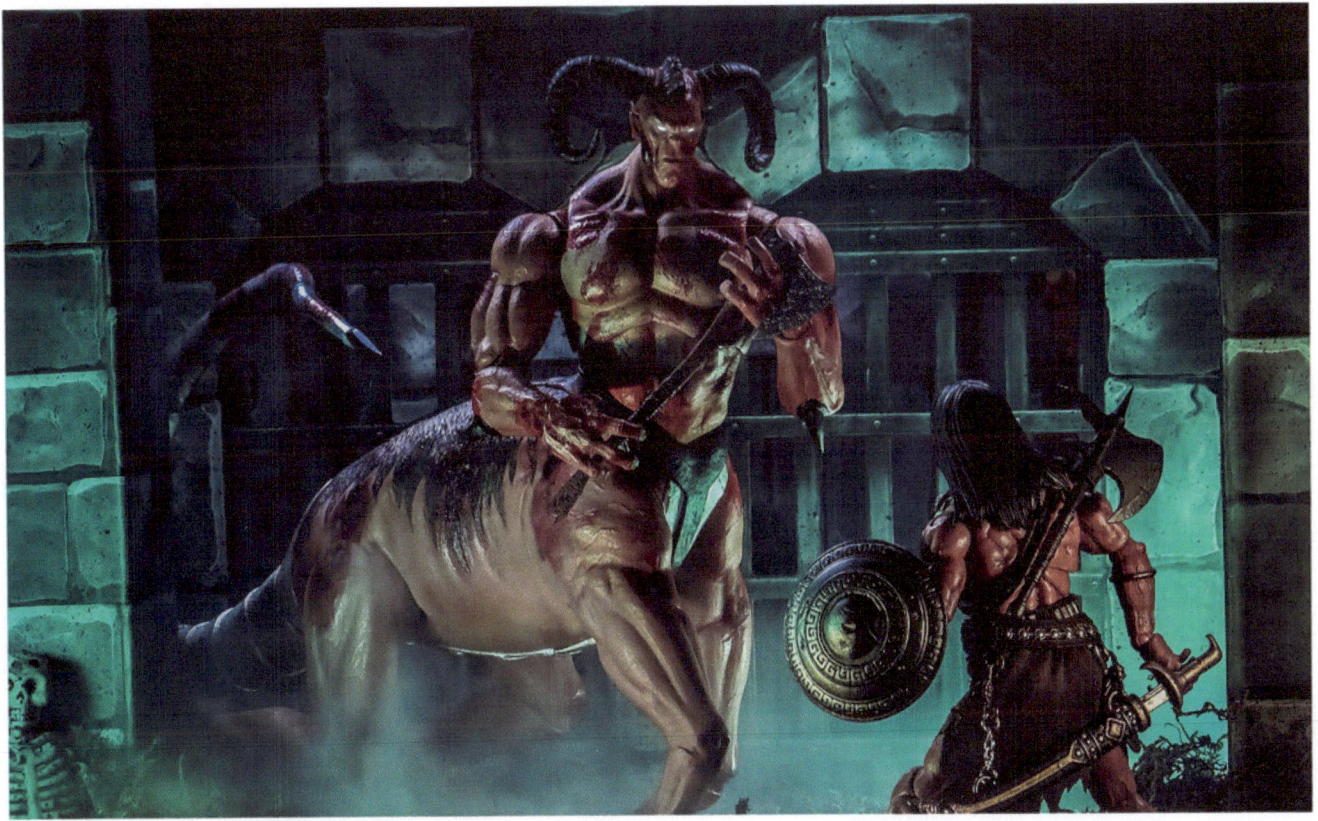

"Run from me and I shall tear apart the mountains to find you" - The Barbarian - **@t_nomad.96**

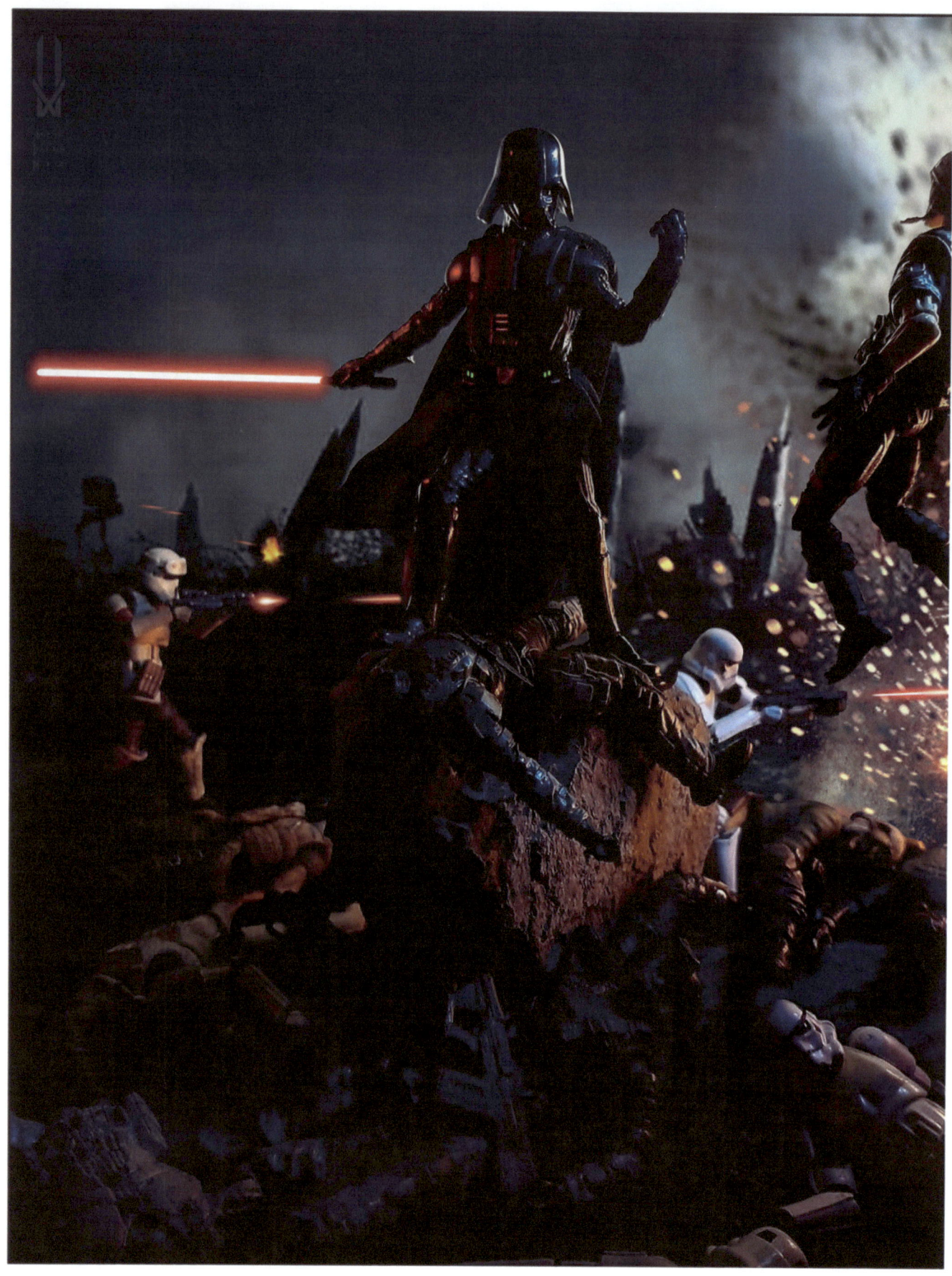

I got impressed with toy photography, and there is where my hobby started, always thinking, (even when I'm working, jeje) of new epic scenes, with my favorite characters doing what I would like to see in live action movies/series. - @Darthwich

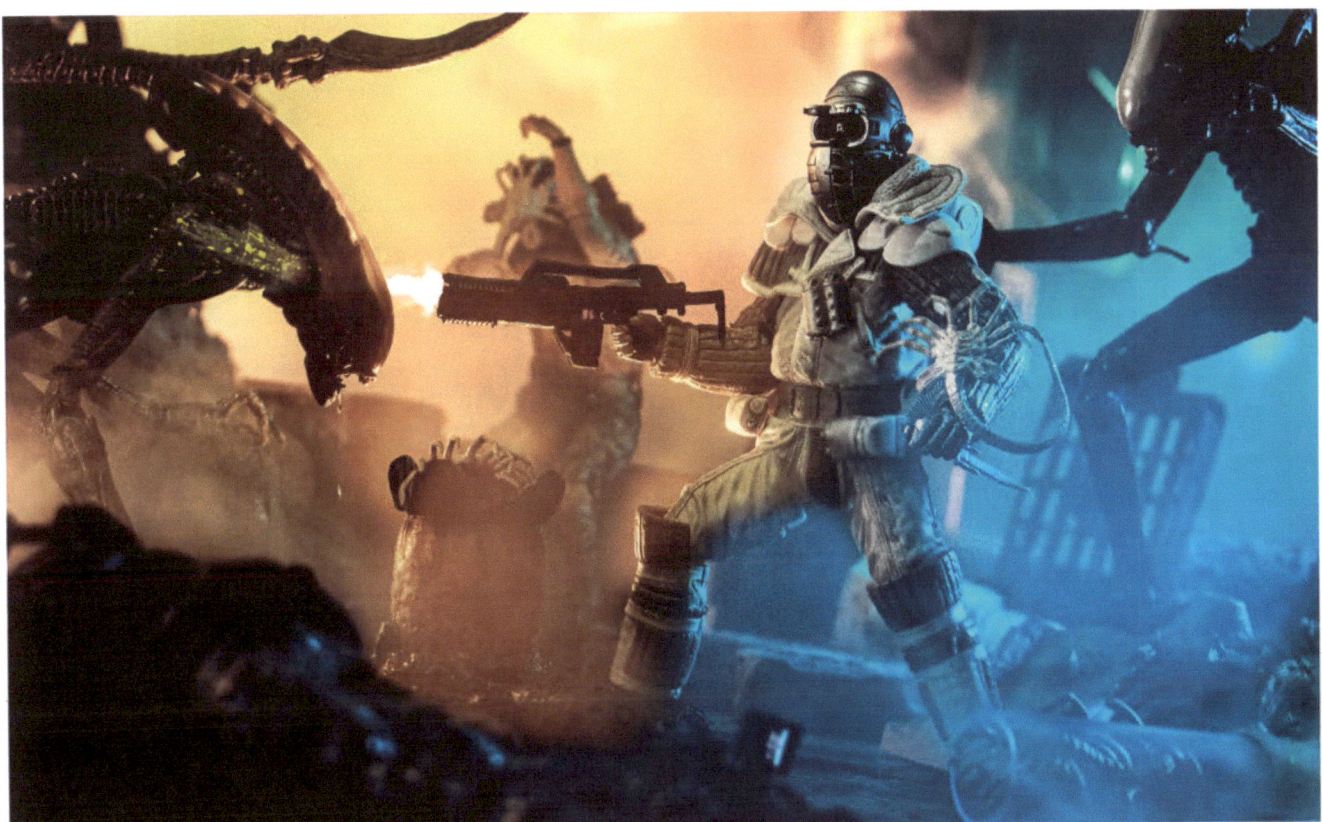

I'd been trying to get ahold of this figure for a number of years - it's one of my favourite designs from the Alien franchise, and I think it's rather underrated. Needless to say, the moment I got it, I was already planning my first shot, which you can see here! - **@UmbraToyPhotos**

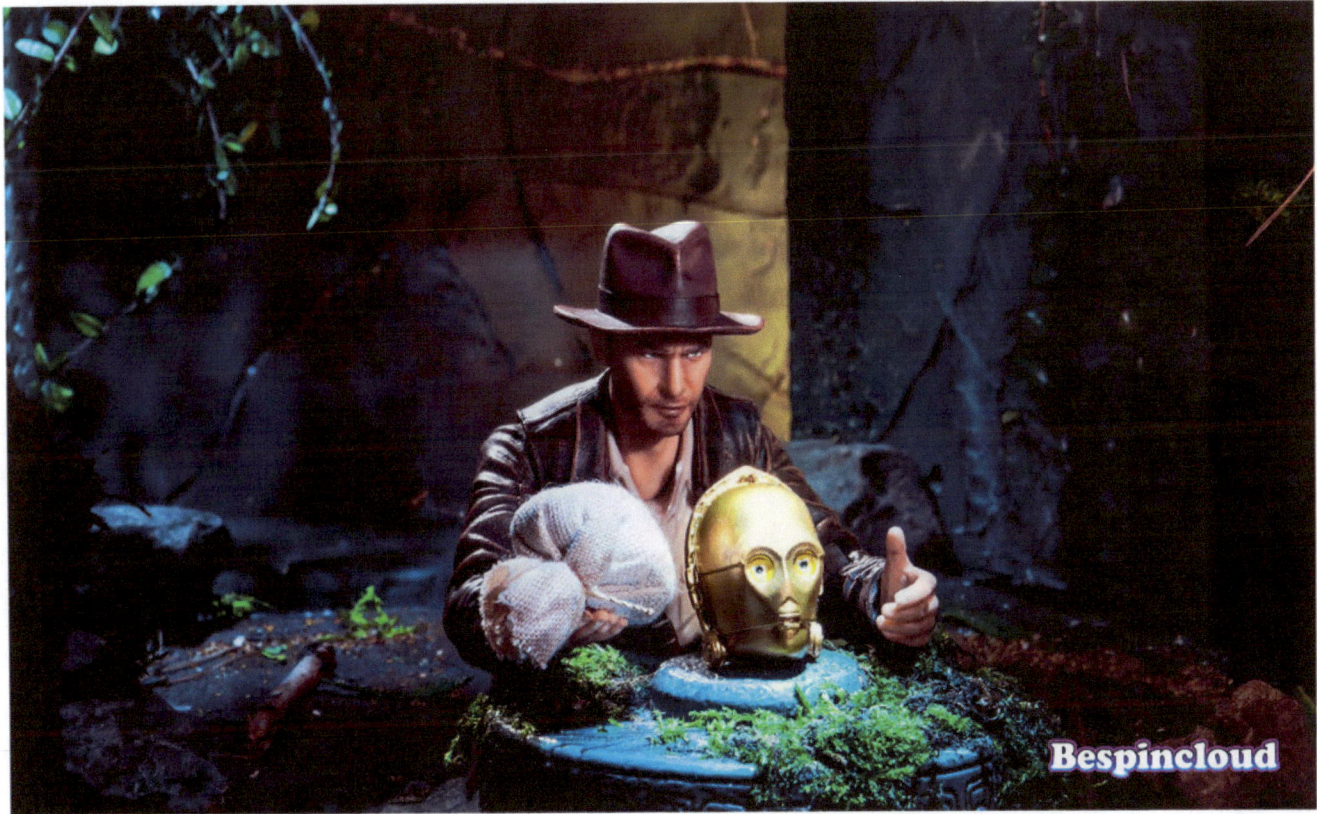

Raiders of the lost droid - **@Bespincloud**

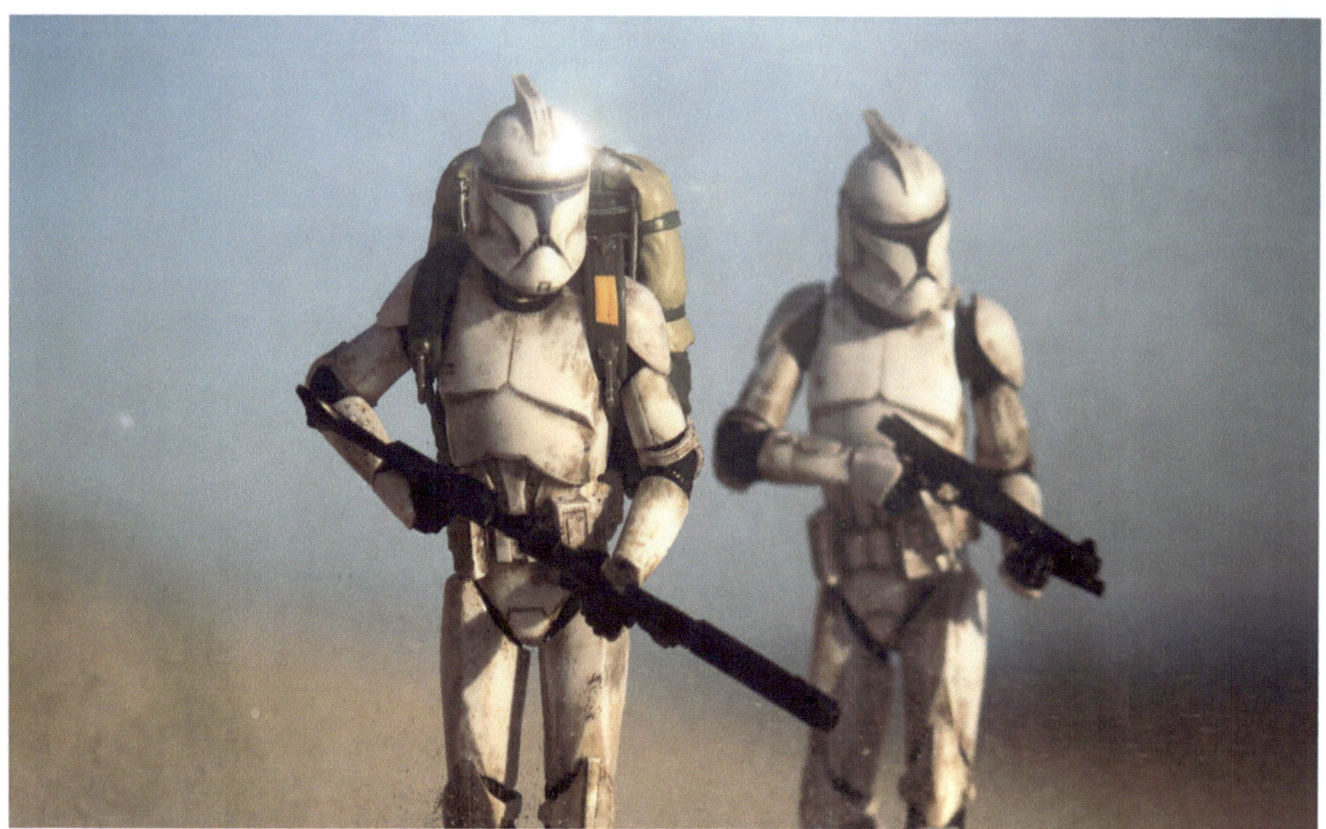

*In this captivating image created by me, one delves deep into the world of Star Wars: The Clone Wars. At the center are two Phase I clone troopers, brought to life through skillful editing and expert positioning. My attention to detail is reflected in every fiber of this scene. - **@phoenix_toyphotography***

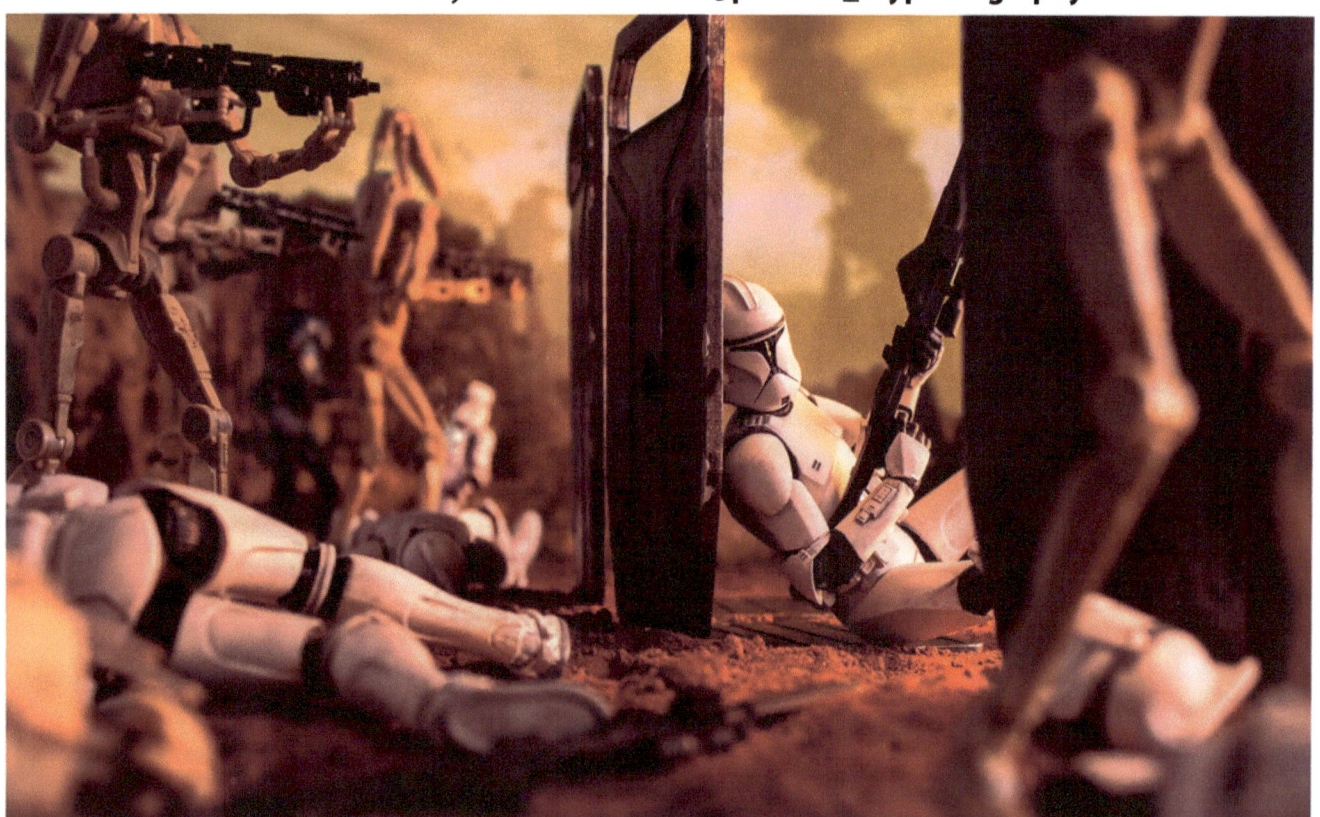

*One of my favourite digirama shots, a mixture of real and digital. When I was shooting this, I felt like a director in a mini version of The Volume. - **@mrstormtrooperdavis***

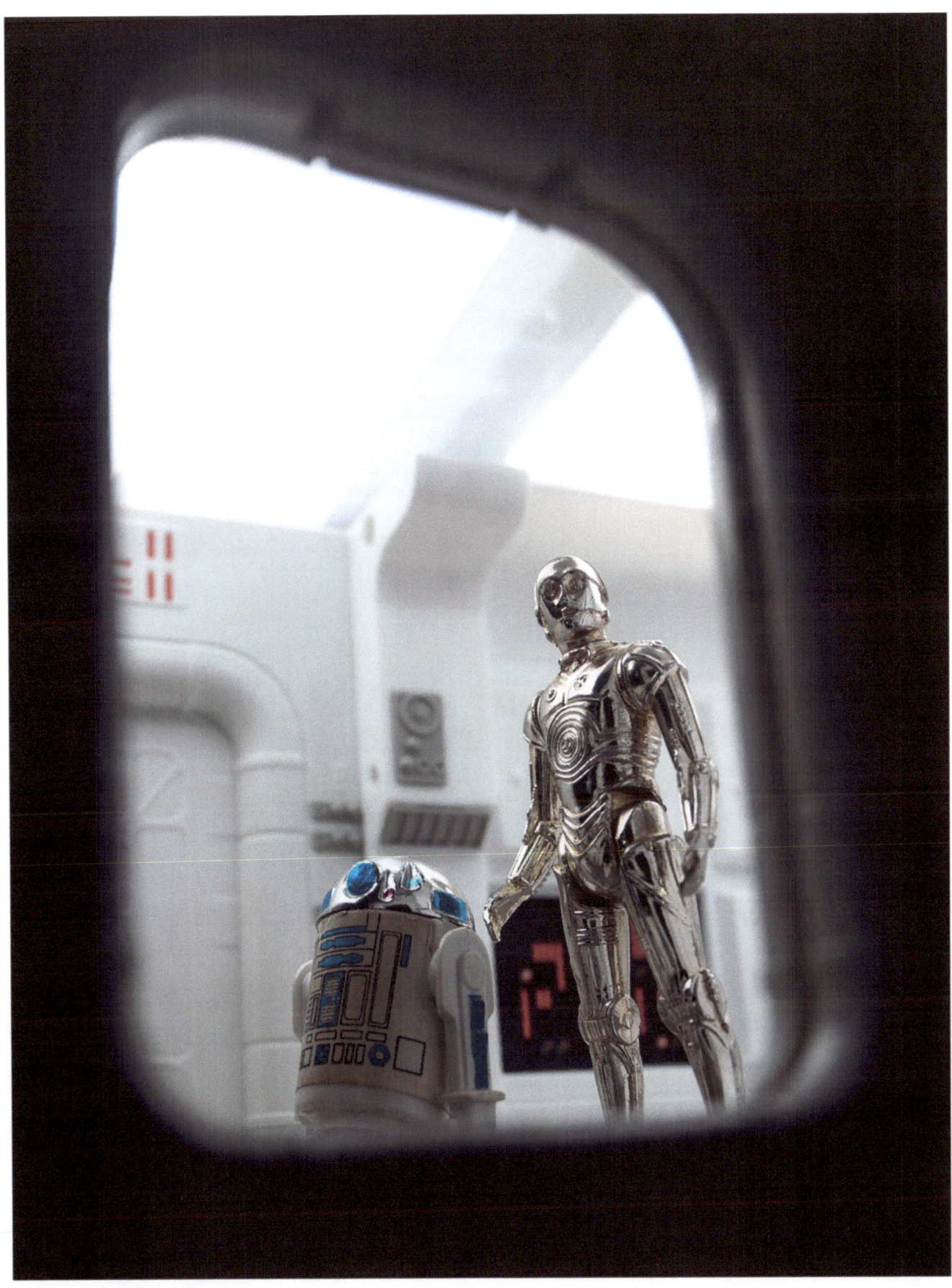

"We're doomed!" - **@3lesie**

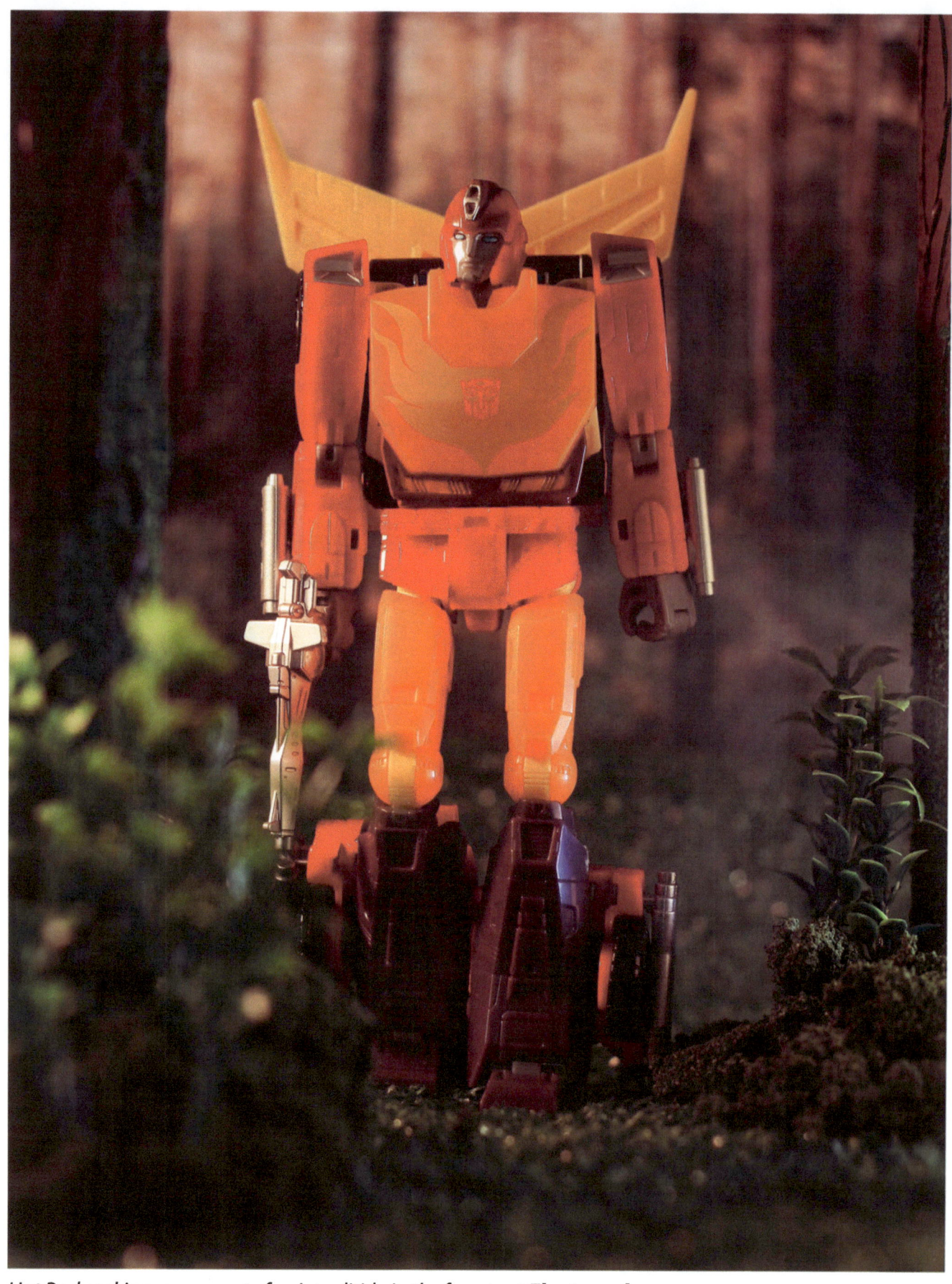

Hot Rod seeking a moment of quiet solitide in the forest. - **@Electrc__dreamer**

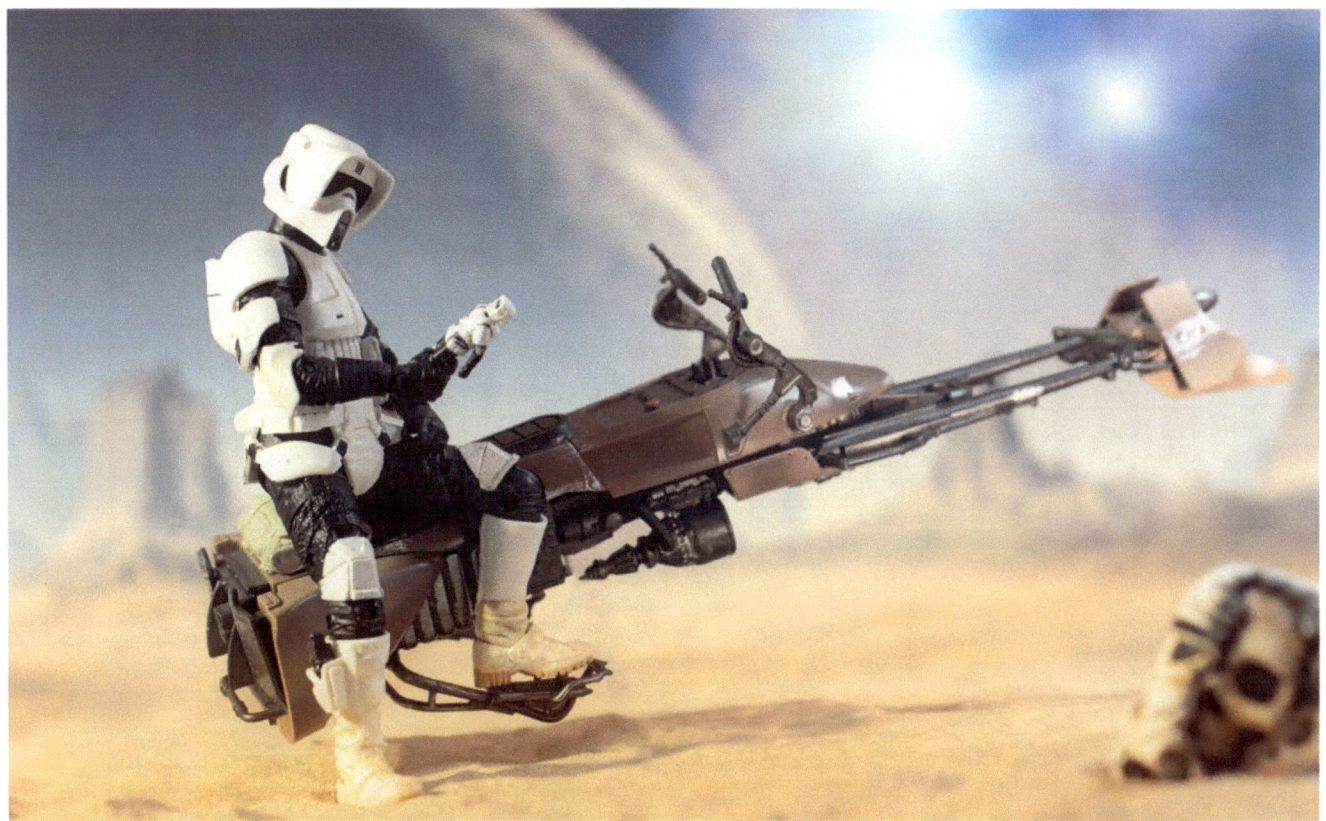

A lost toy... For this photo I used a backdrop for the background and some kinetic sand, this scout trooper seems pensive in front of the toy in his likness found in the desert... I like to hope that he's thinking about the consequences of the war and the suffering endured by the population... - @wookierevenge

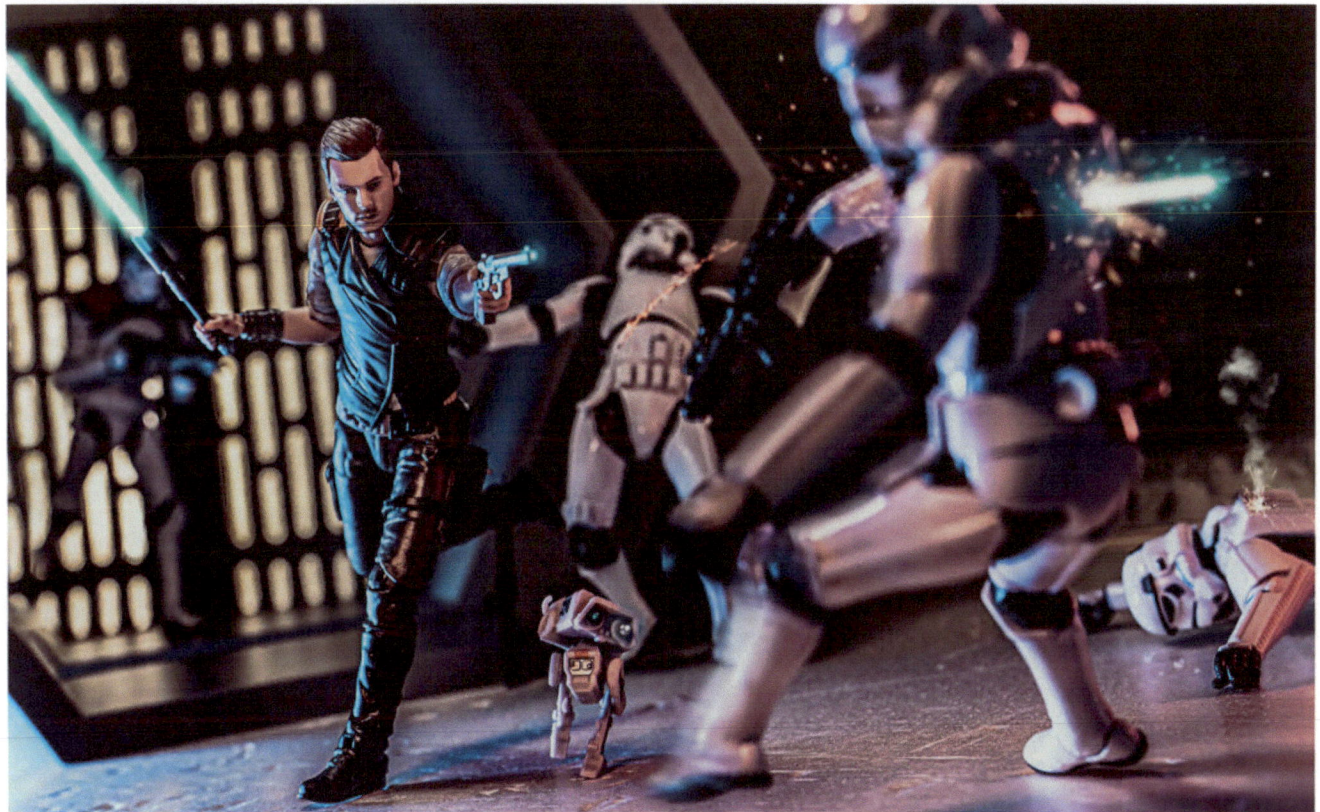

*I've been collecting figurines in their boxes since 2012. When I discovered toy photography in 2020, it was a revelation! I have to take them out of their boxes to bring them to life! - @_visual_horizon_*

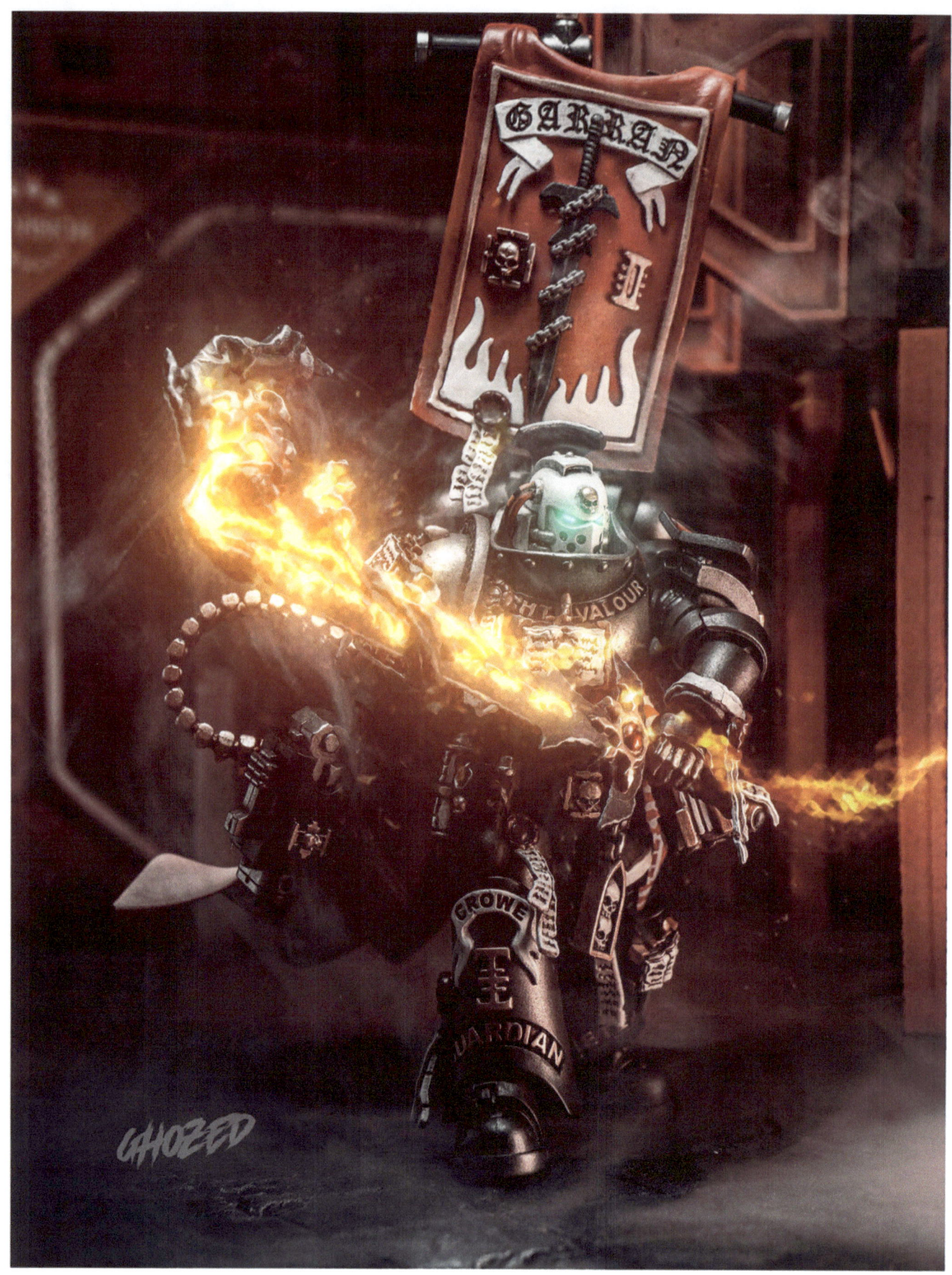

*I am the warden of the blade - @**gh0zed***

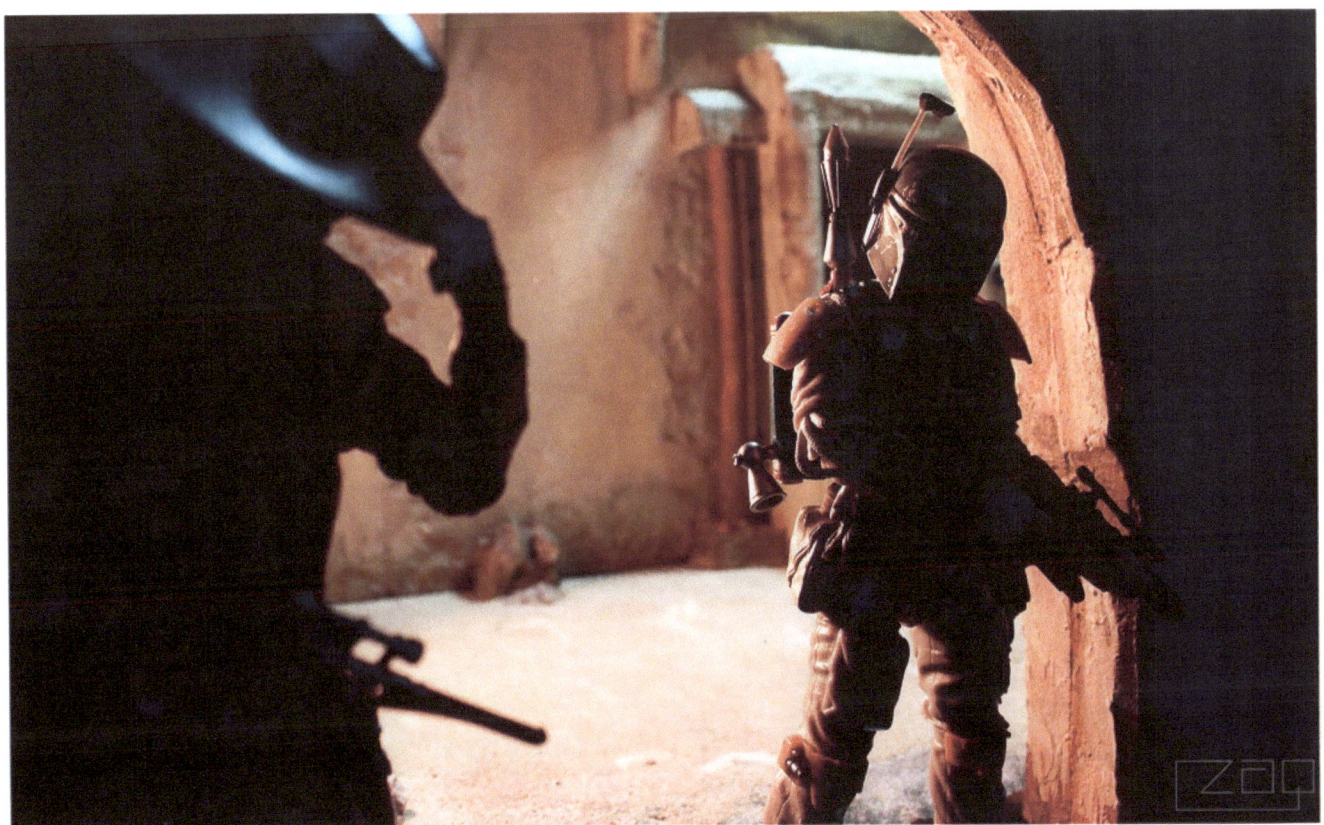

"I'm your huckleberry" - **@Zaqtionfigures**

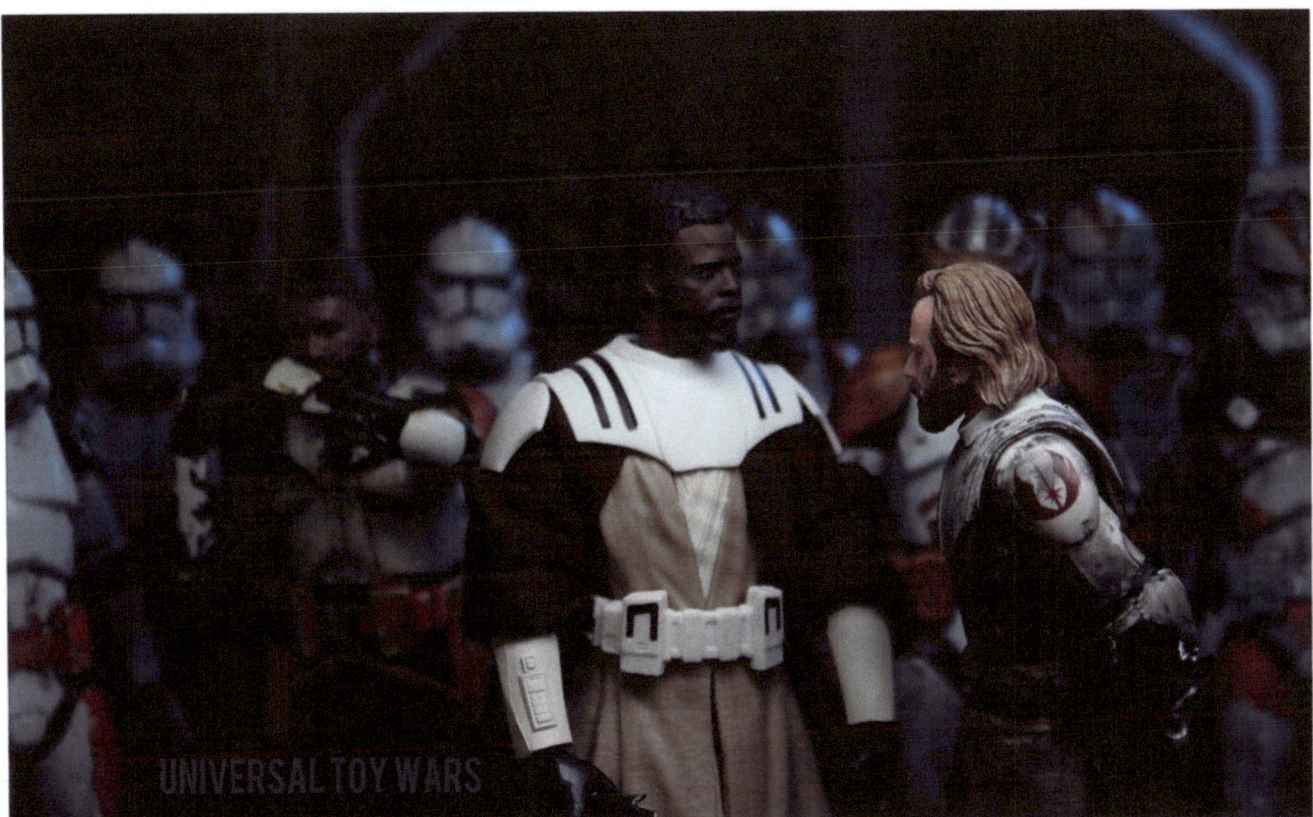

Jedi Masters Baric Talis and Obi-Wan Kenobi: One of my most recent shots that I am extremely proud of. The opportunity to create stories in this vast and beautiful universe gives me a great sense of community and belonging. - **@UniversalToyWars**

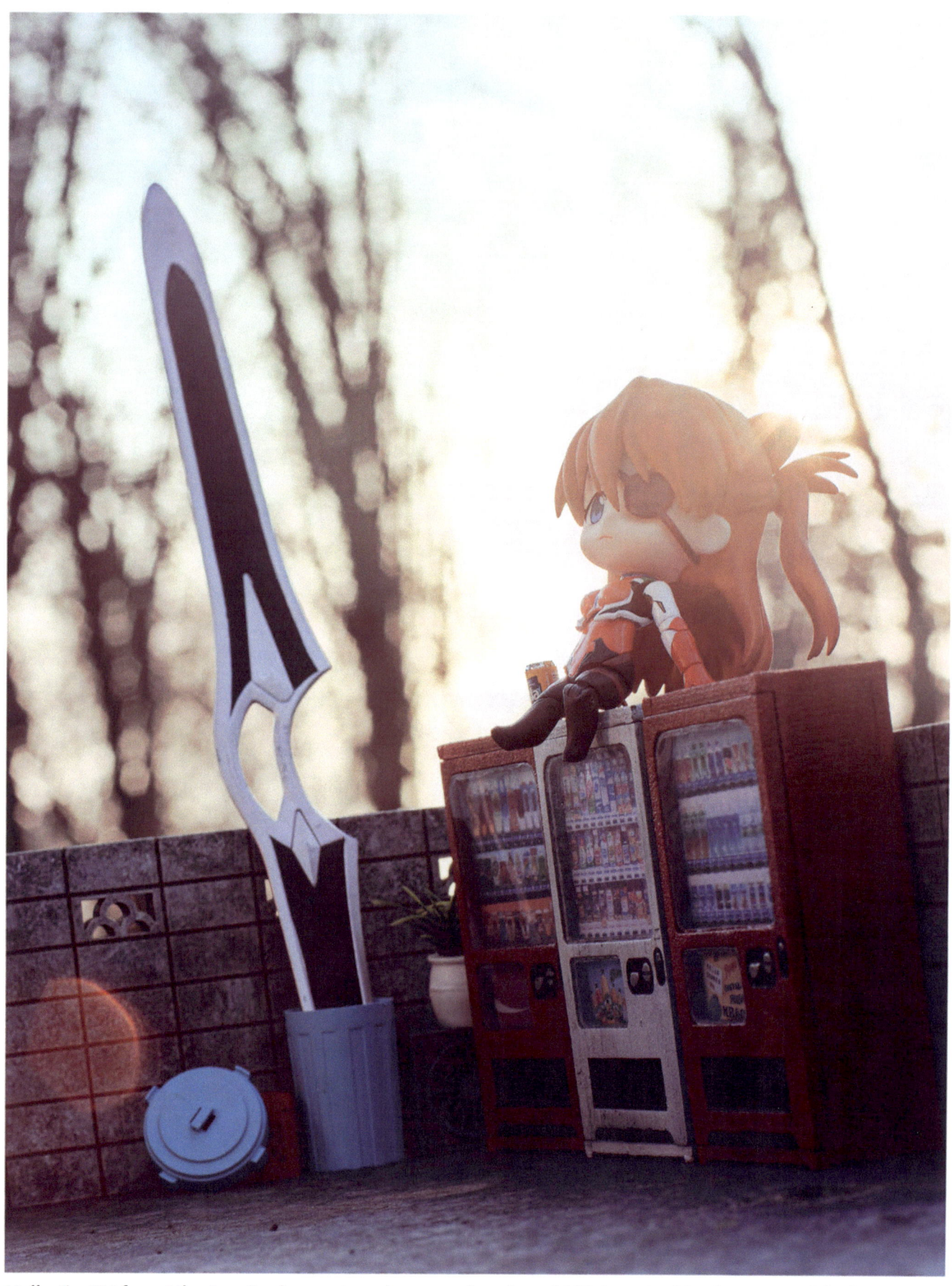

Hello, I'm Tei from Ukraine. I've been a toy photographer since 2017. I made this photo a week before russian full-scale invasion in Ukraine. Previous book helped my country, so I join for a good cause.
- **@teissonh**

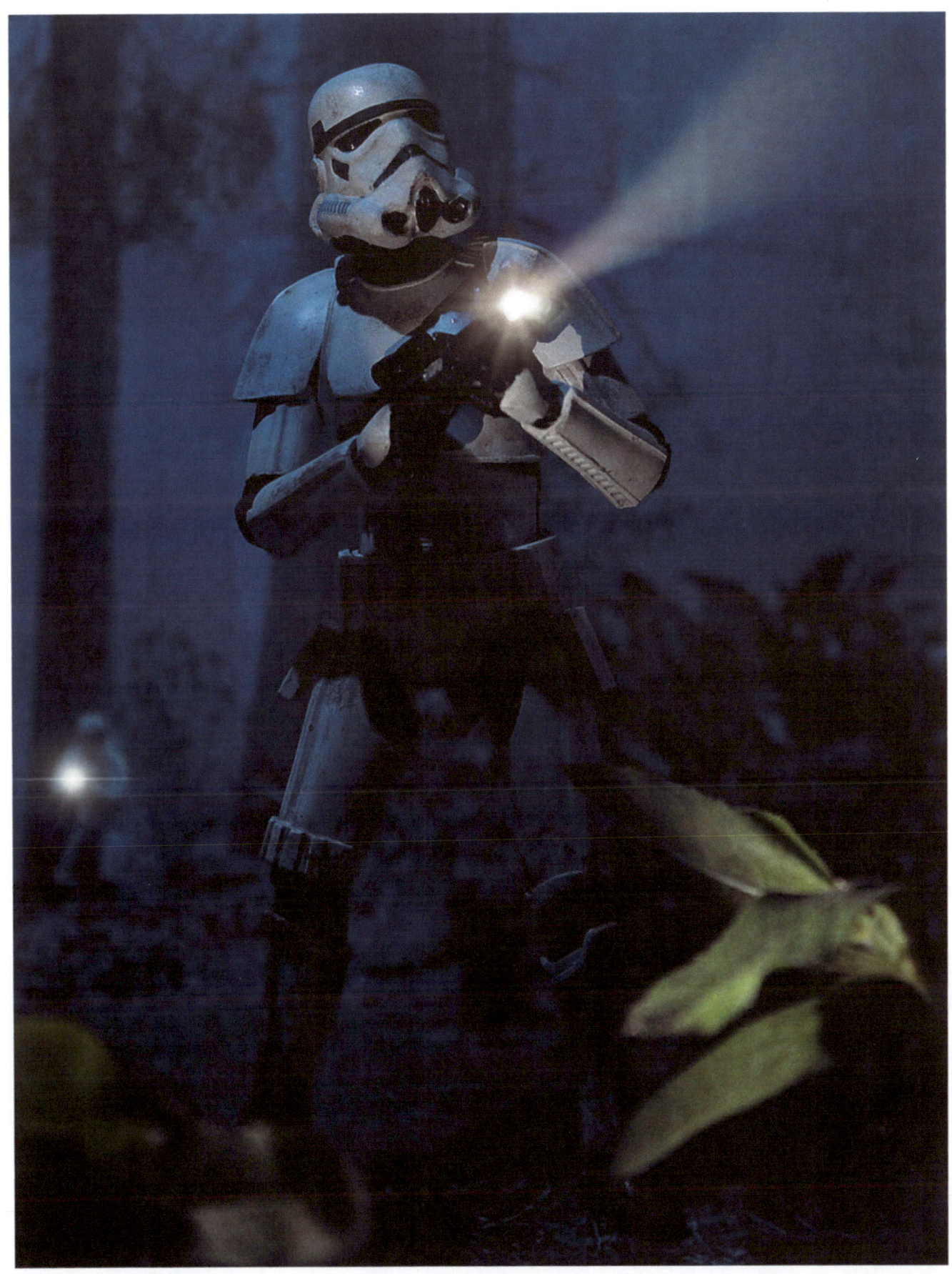

Love the subtle differences from all the different stormtrooper costumes especially the ROTJ trooper armour which was 3D scanned in for Battlefront 1 & 2, so much so the on screen models are 100% accurate to the props, something i wanted to make in 1/12 - @gi_trooper_kits

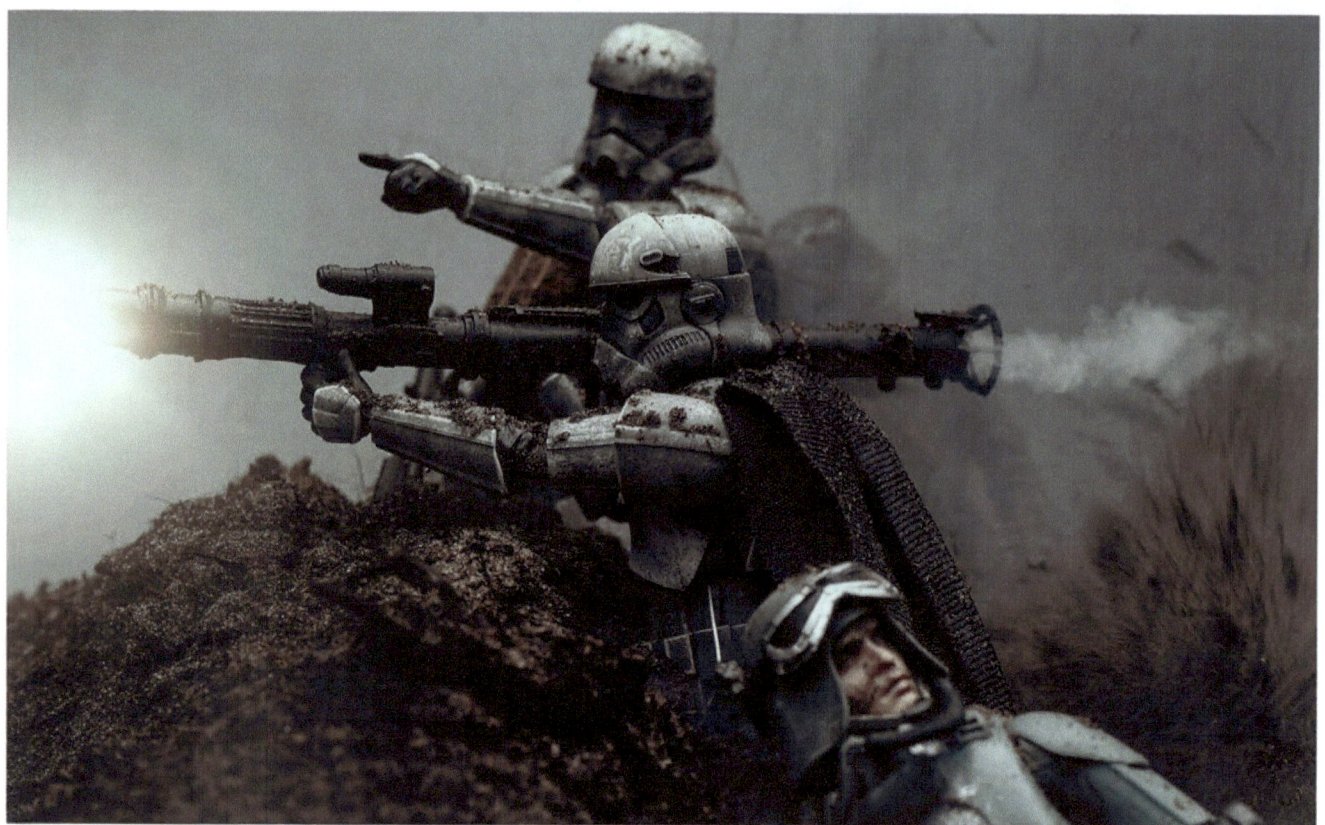

This photo is my take of a photo I have seen of British Marines fighting in a recent conflict. I really love the gritty feel of the Mimban war in Star Wars and tried to combine the image and the film.
- @Agalaxyfarfarfaraway

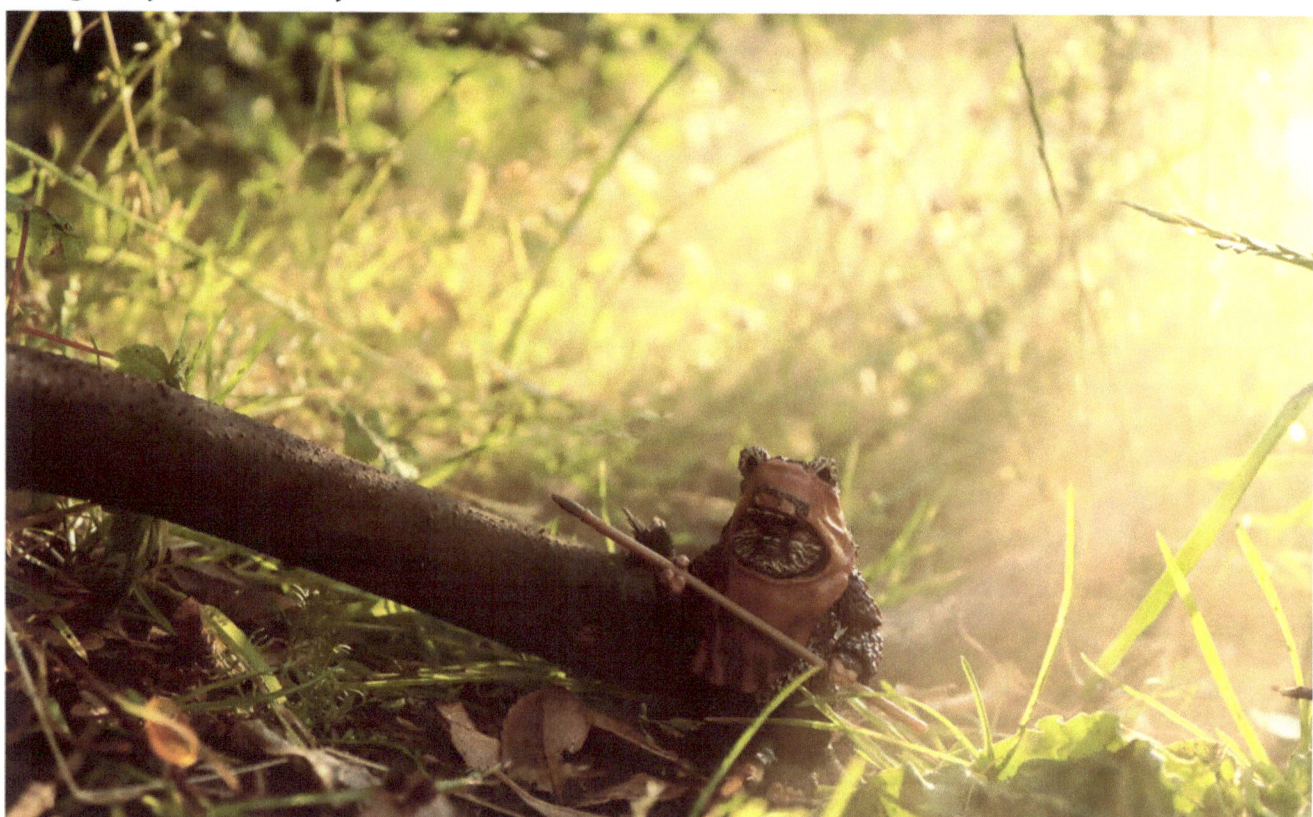

Sunset patrol on Endor - Fun fact: Warwick Davis has a copy of this photograph, gifted to him at Liverpool Comic Con. - **@Geeky_gifts_by_j_and_m**

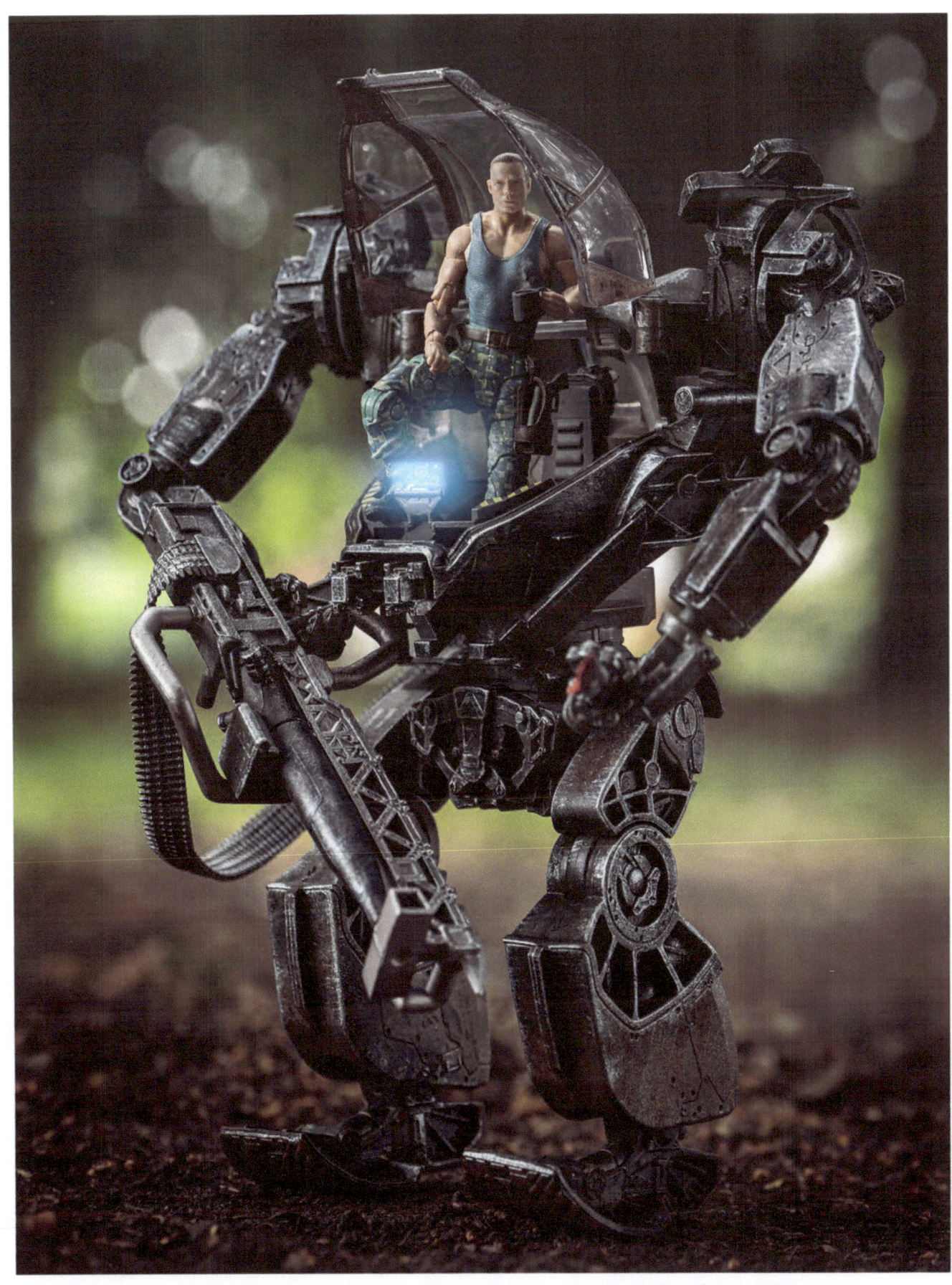

A marine can't be defeated. Oh, you can kill us, but we'll just regroup in hell! - **@frame_the_toys**

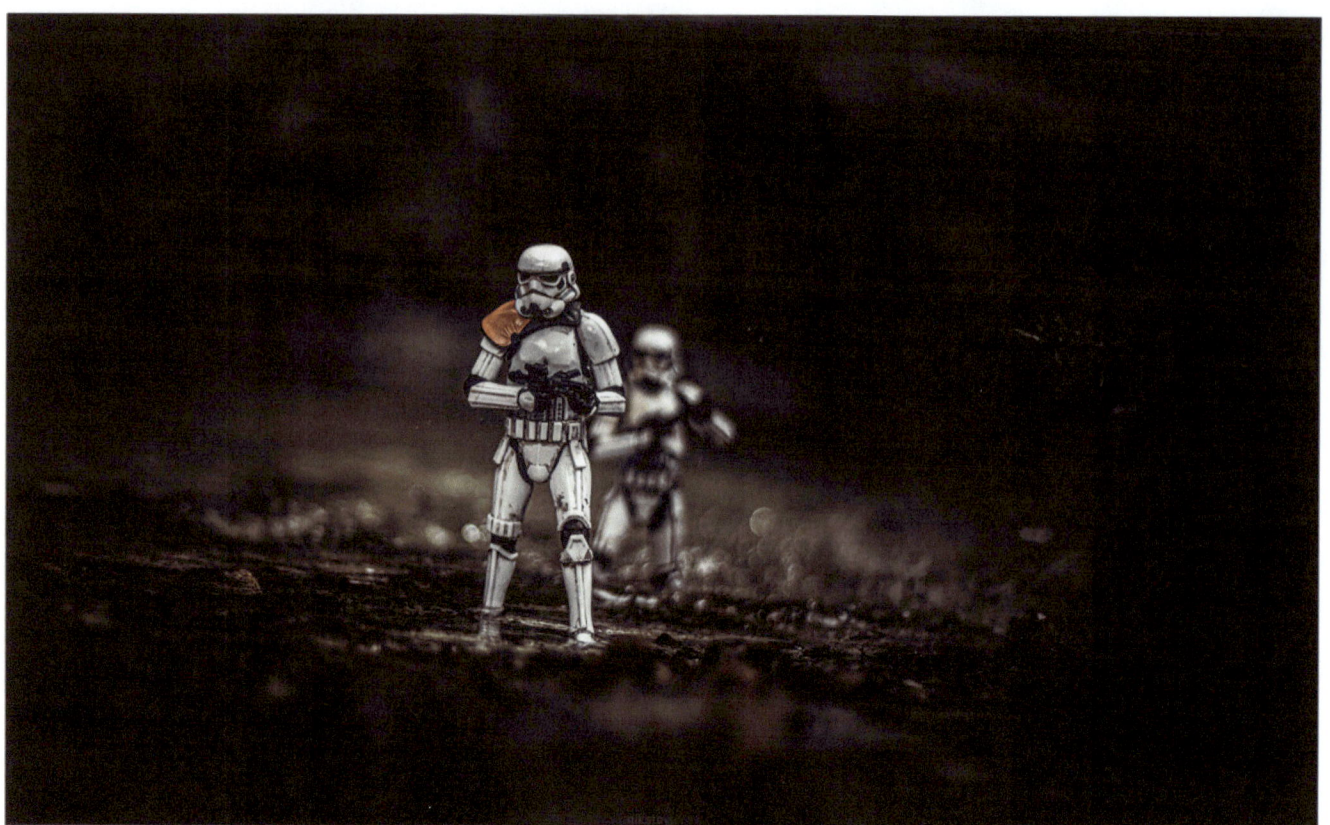

This photo was taken on my trip to Costa Rica a few years ago. I look back on it quite fondly. I've always liked to photograph my figures in natural and grandiose locations, adding a sense of scale and realism.
 - **@nikstoypicss**

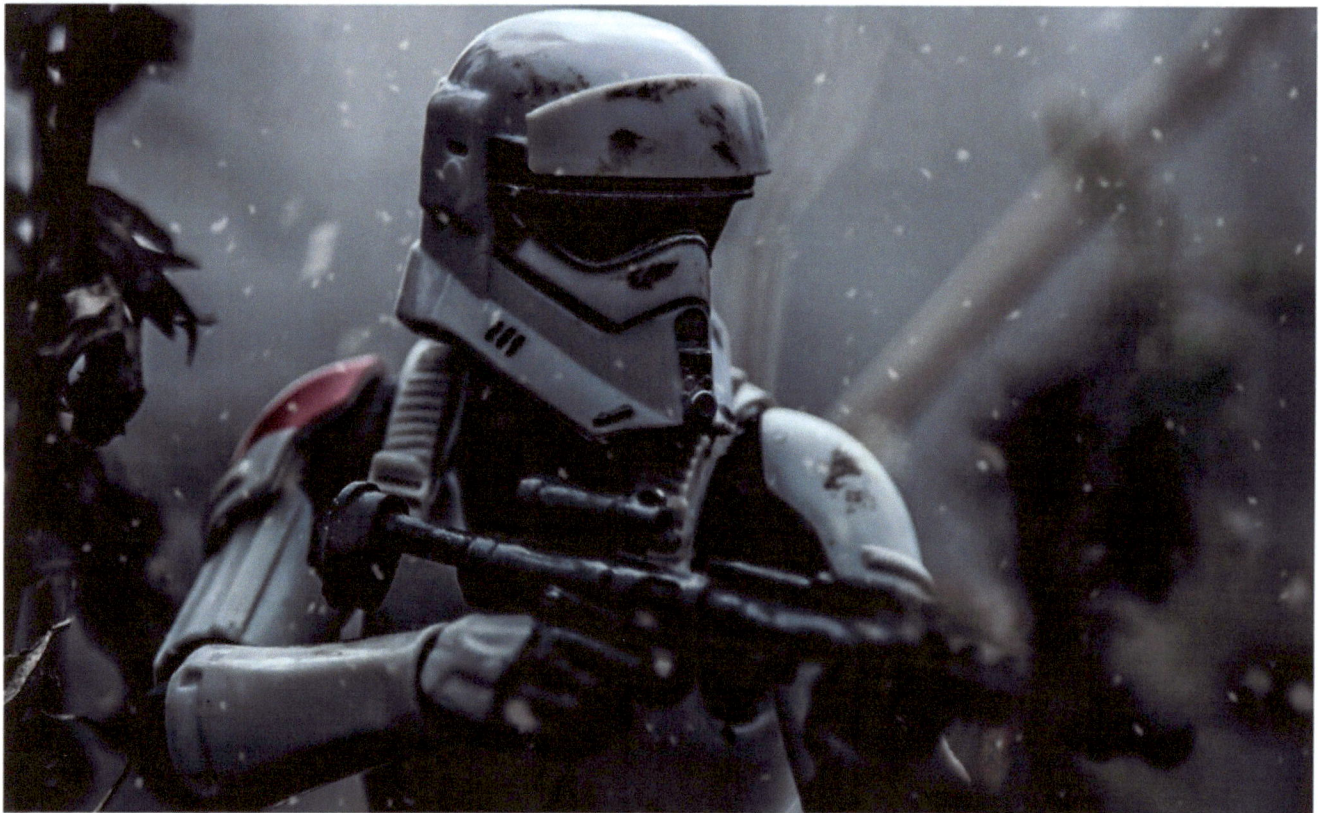

War must be, while we defend our lives against a destroyer who would devour all; but I do not love the bright sword for its sharpness, nor the warrior for his glory. I love only that which they defend.
- **@mm_studi0s**

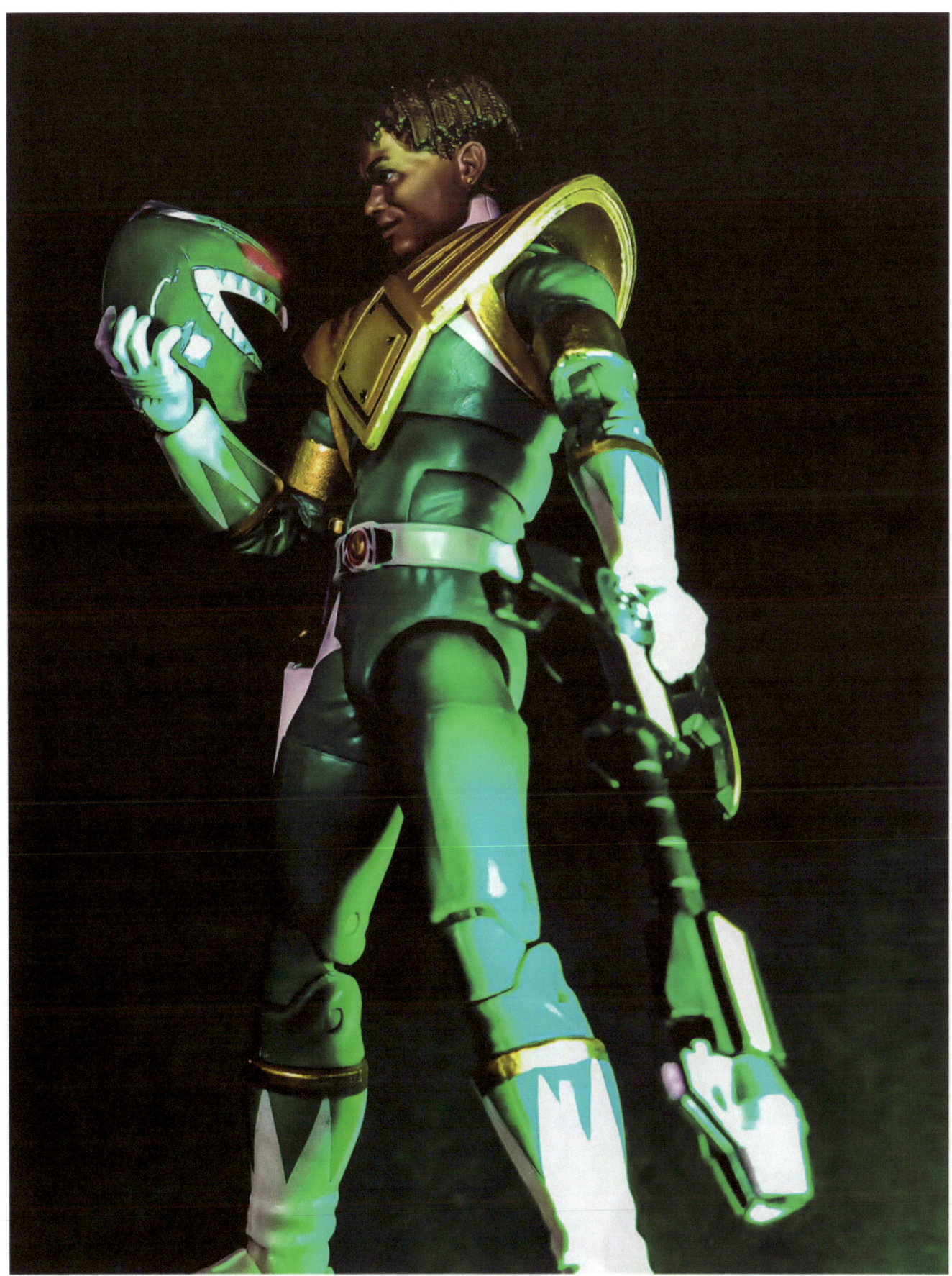

I wanted to do a what if scenario for power rangers. Growing up I was a huge fan of Zack the original black ranger and I felt like he never got enough recognition. So, this is my tribute to the love I have for the character and the series as a whole. **- @jhonnyrhino**

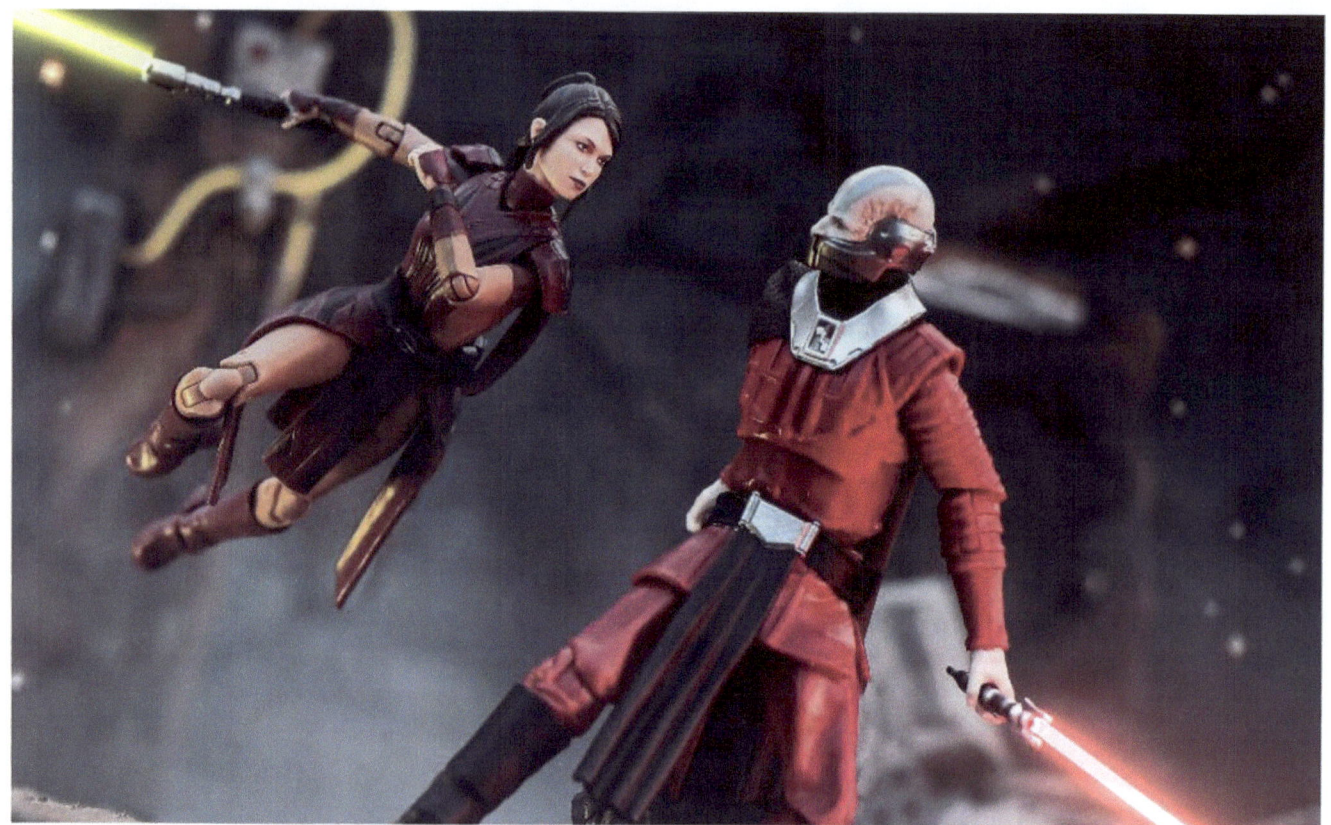

A classic struggle between good and evil. Absolutely love these characters from the KOTOR series. Very simple setup and used natural light outside. - @850SithLord

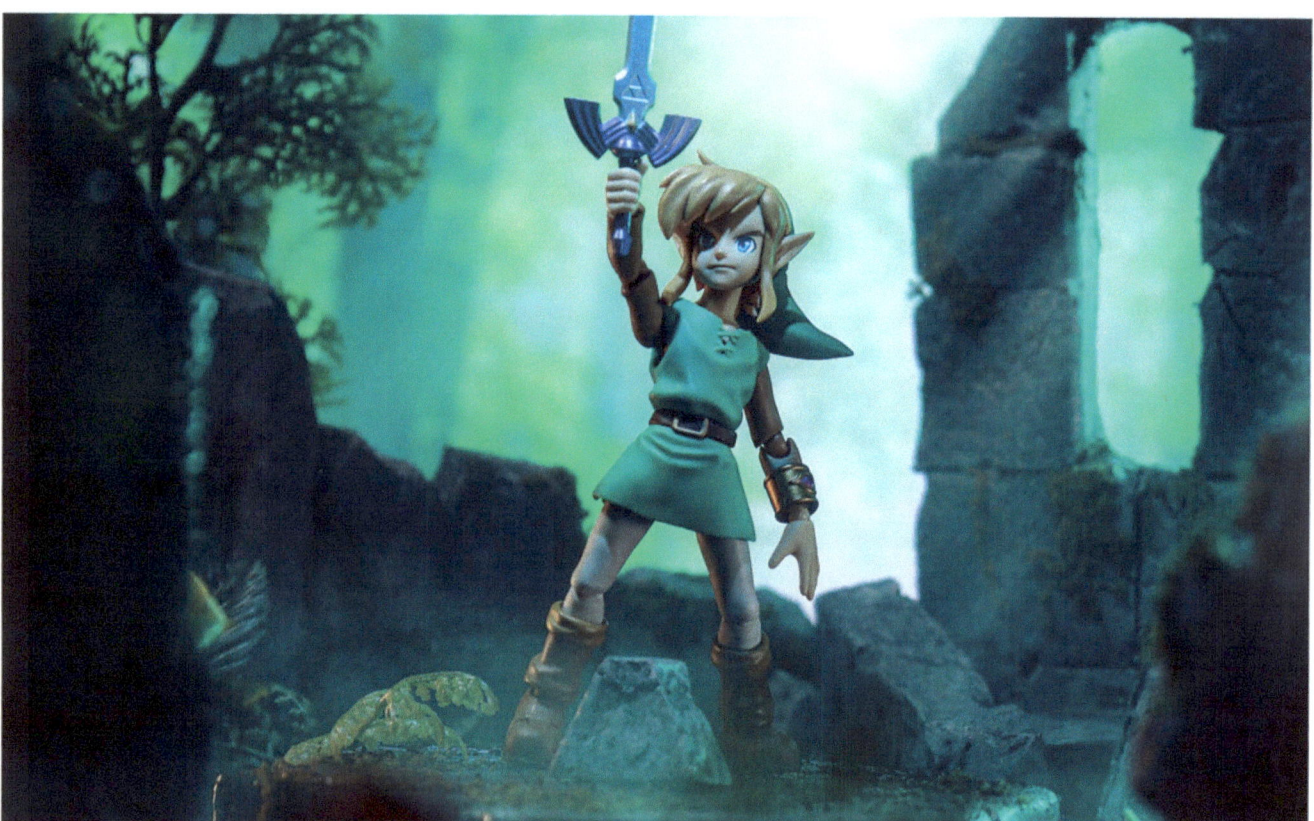

Time passes, people move. Like a river's flow, it never ends. A childish mind will turn to noble ambition. Young love will become deep affection. The clear water's surface reflects growth. - @Intergalactic_raptor

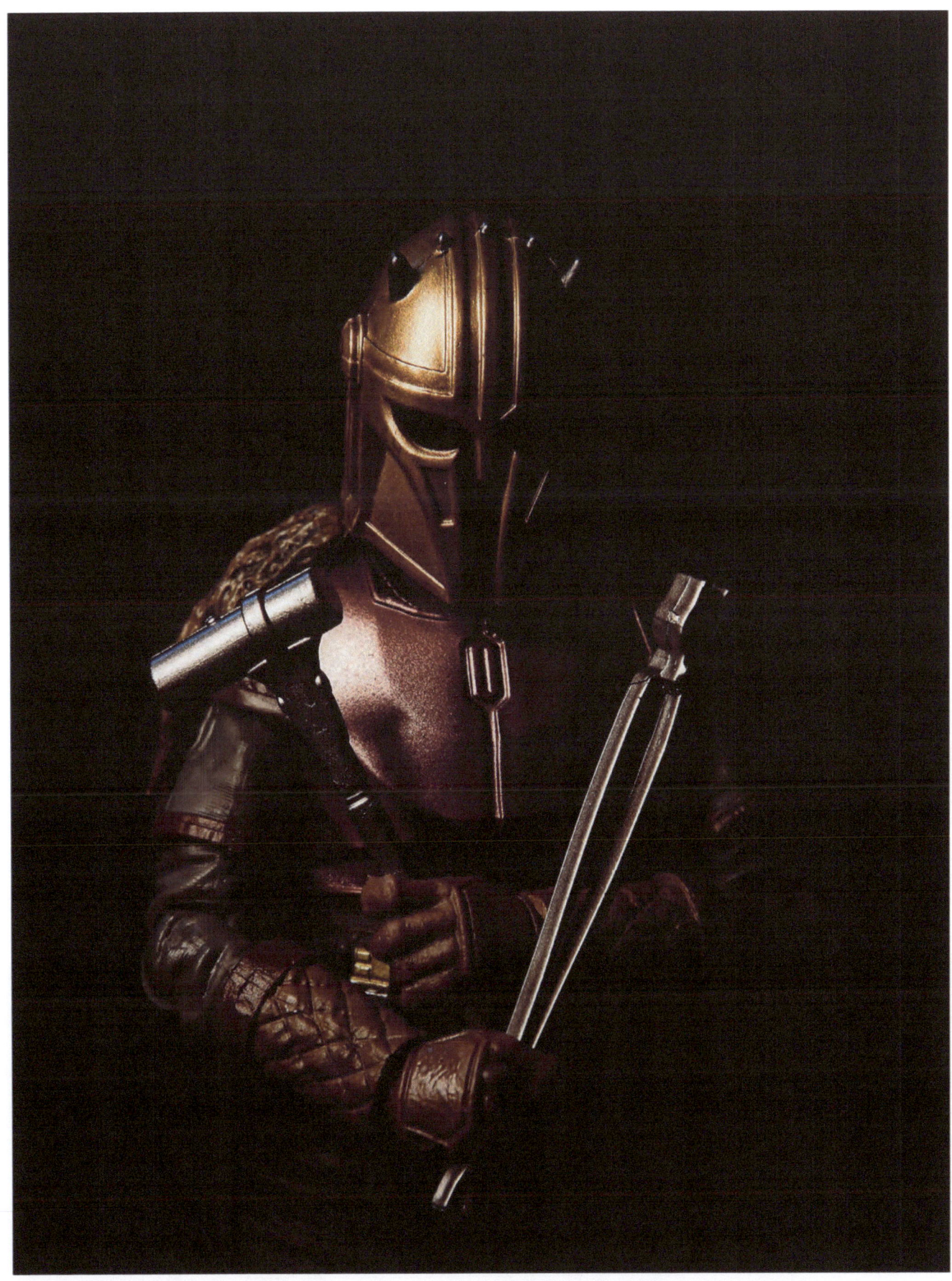

The Mysterious Armorer from the Mandalorian. Shot using techniques learnt from the toy photography community, I have been inspired to start a studio series of my favourite figures.

- @Kestis_toy_photography

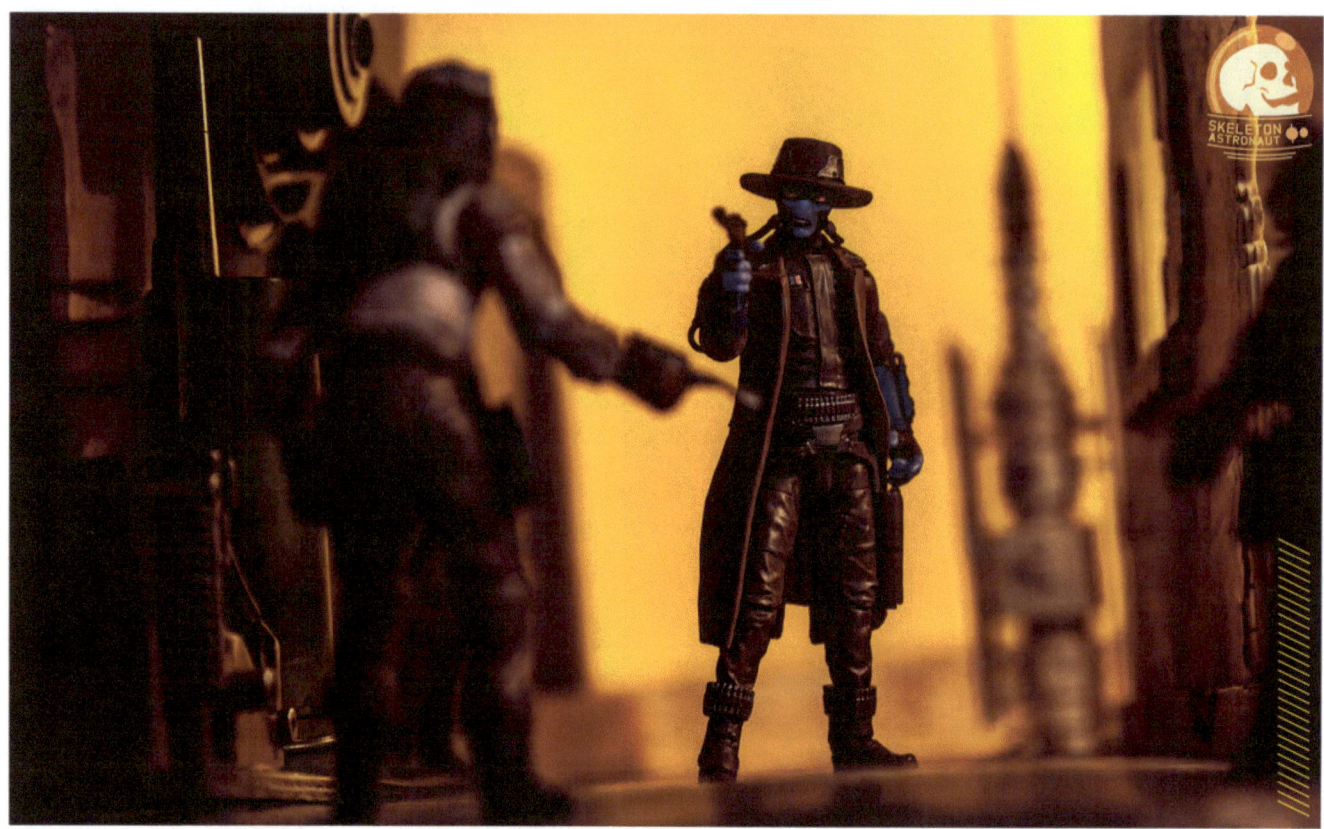

"From the Desert Comes a Stranger" - **@SkeletonAstronaut**

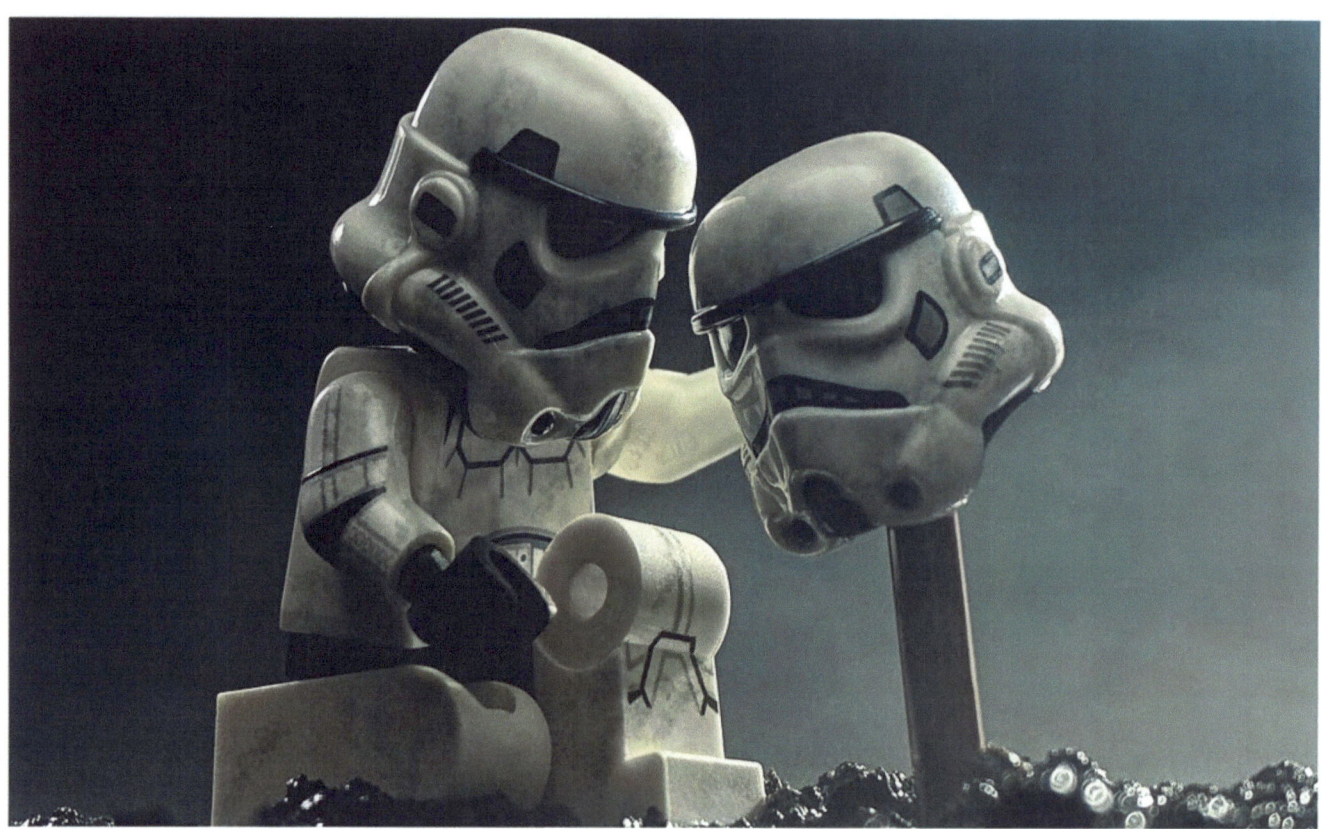

Bon voyage my friend - **@Brickpanda82**

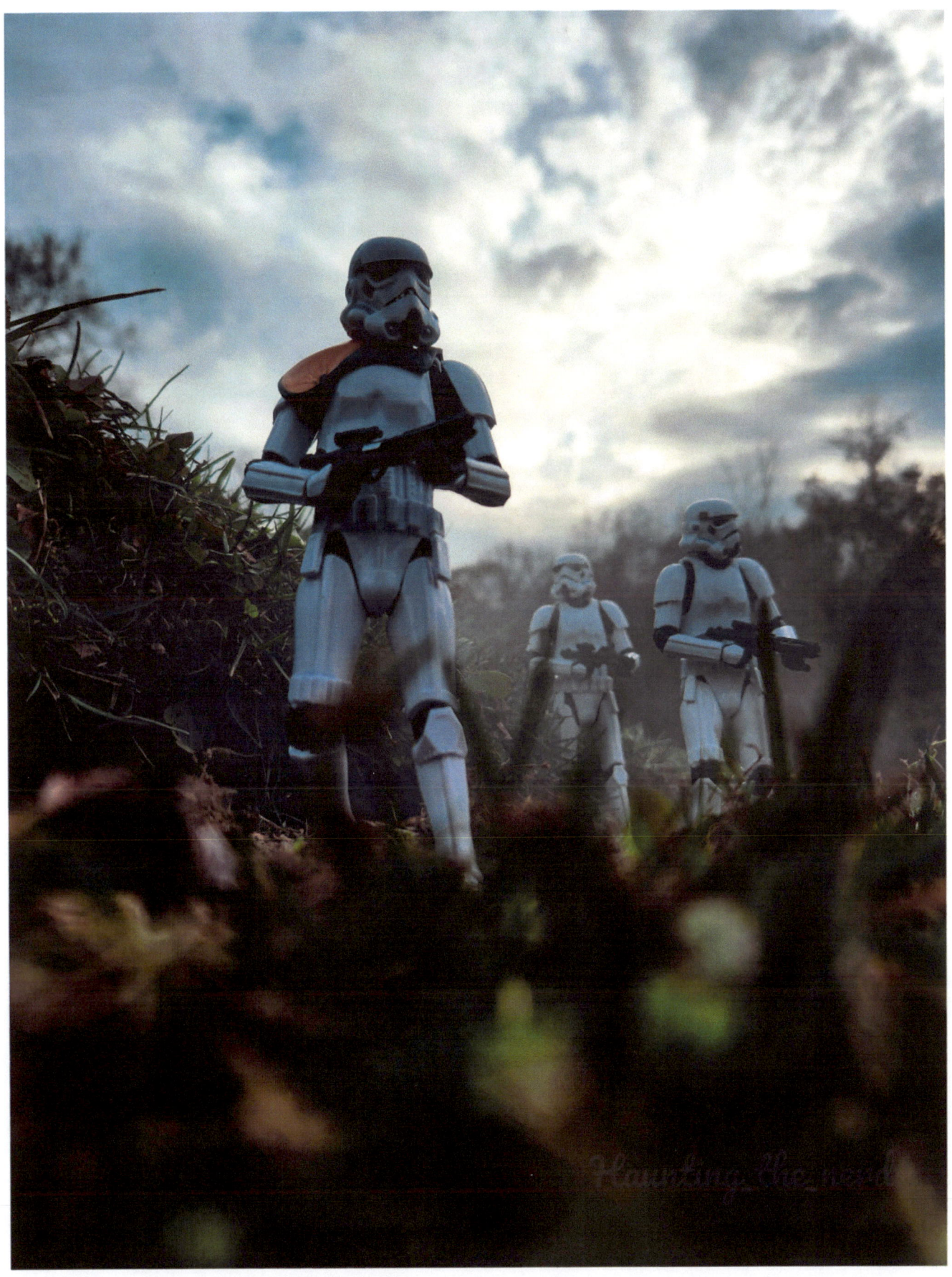

I got into toy photography in 2020, it's something that always interest me. The stories created in a shot, learning new skills and tricks and overall having fun with it. This is truly a great community to be apart of.
- @Haunting_the_nerd

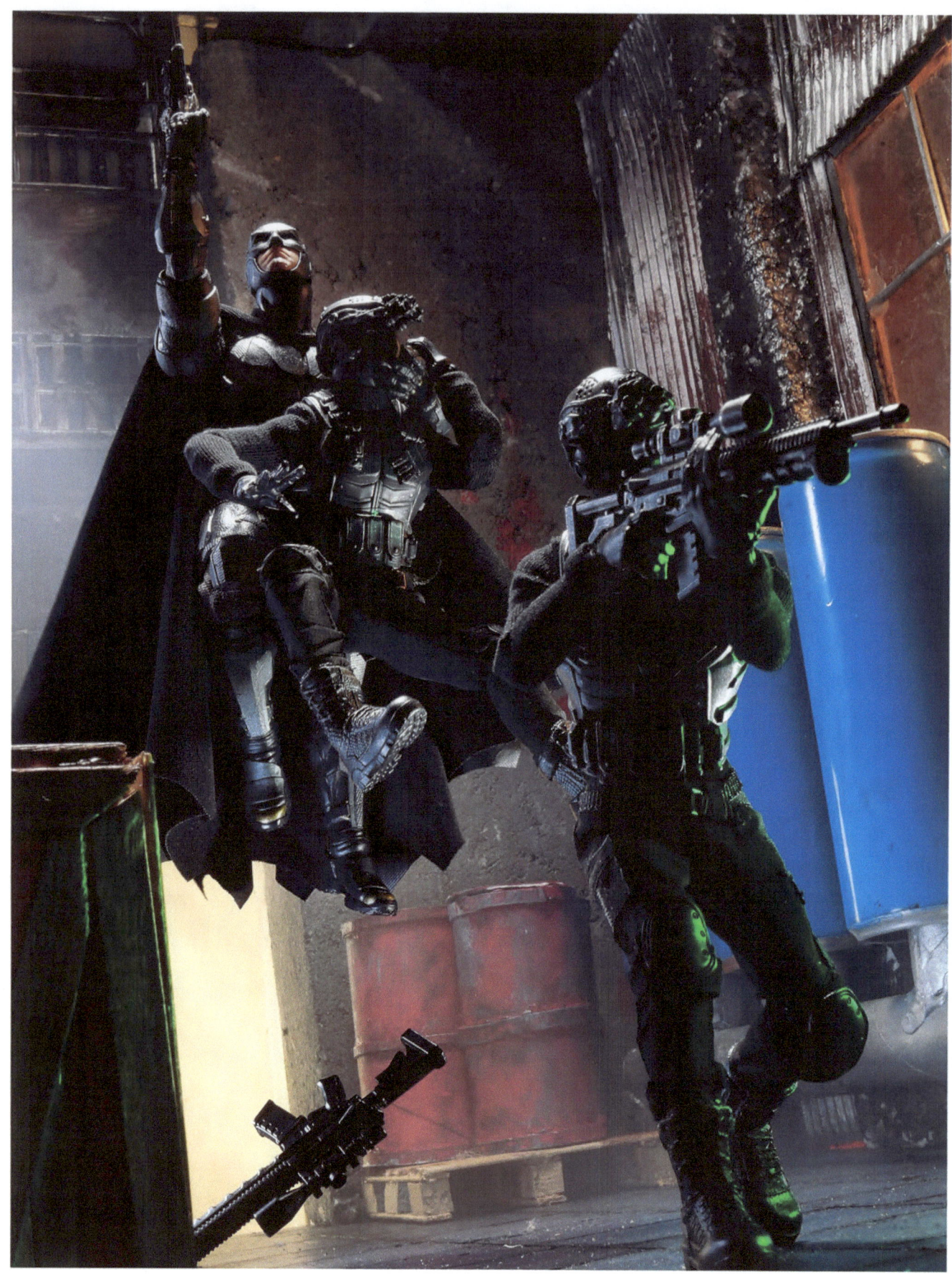

A Silent Knight. - **@kneelbeforezod**

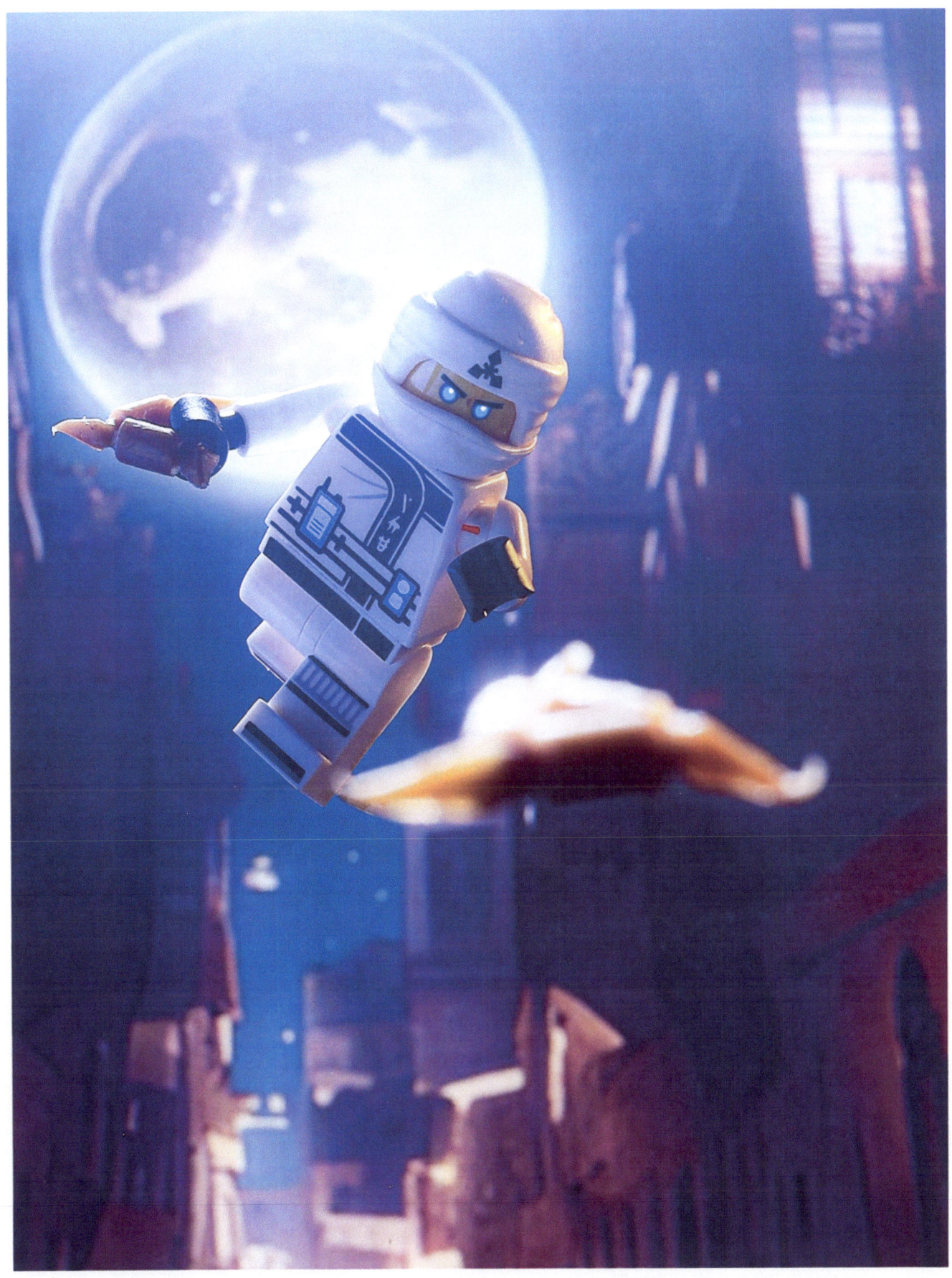

*I grew up watching Ninjago and Zane has always been my favorite from the series. Last year I took similar photo with Zane throwing a ninja star at an enemy. I wanted to redo the photo with some differences and see how I've improved in the year. - **@LDaigle_Photography***

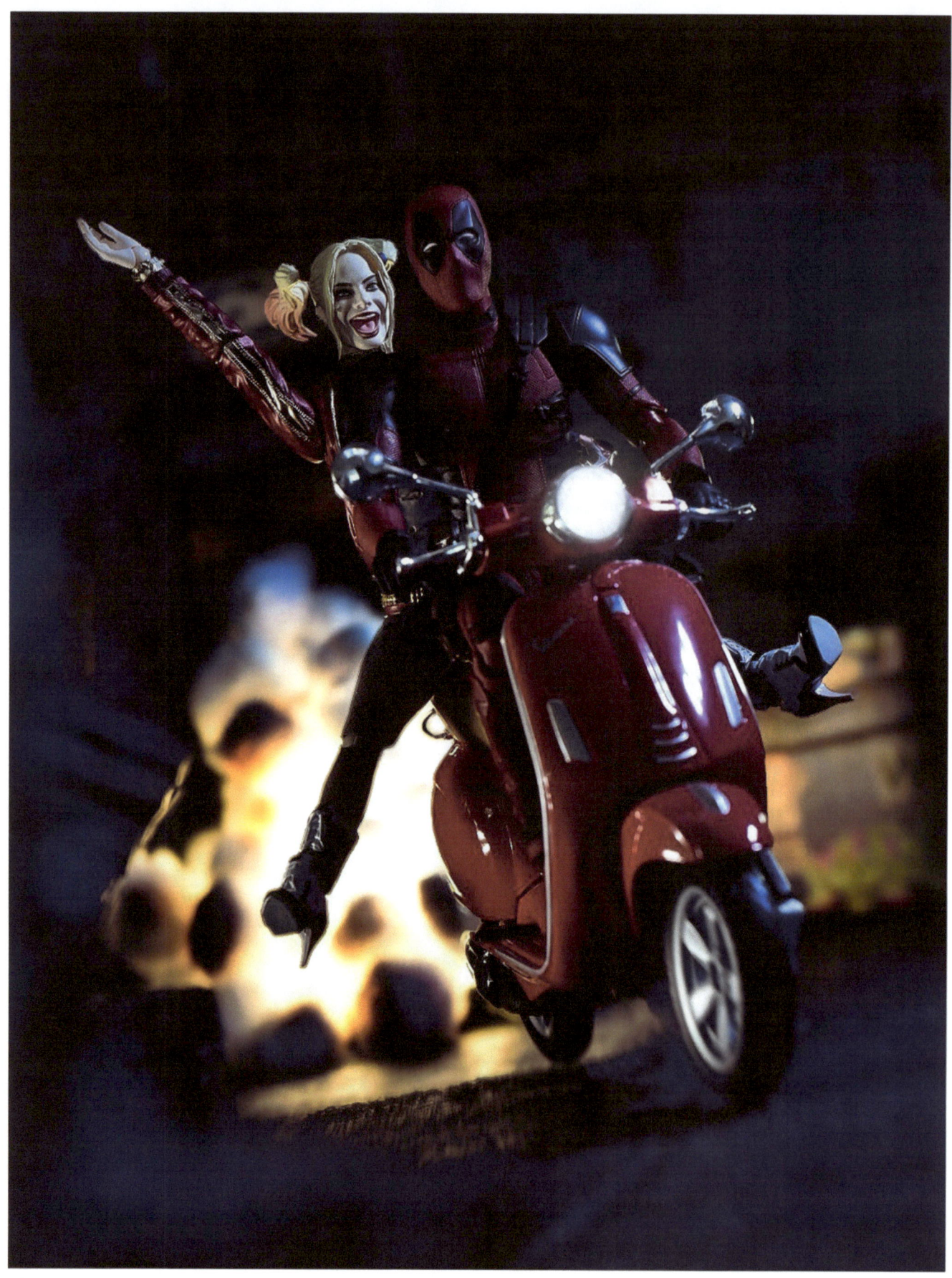

I have had this idea on my bucket list and wanted to execute this shot and get it out there. Here I am sharing it to you guys, and I hope you like it. I think Harleypool would make a perfect couple, since their Crazy matches each other. Don't you think? - **@Litratoyz**

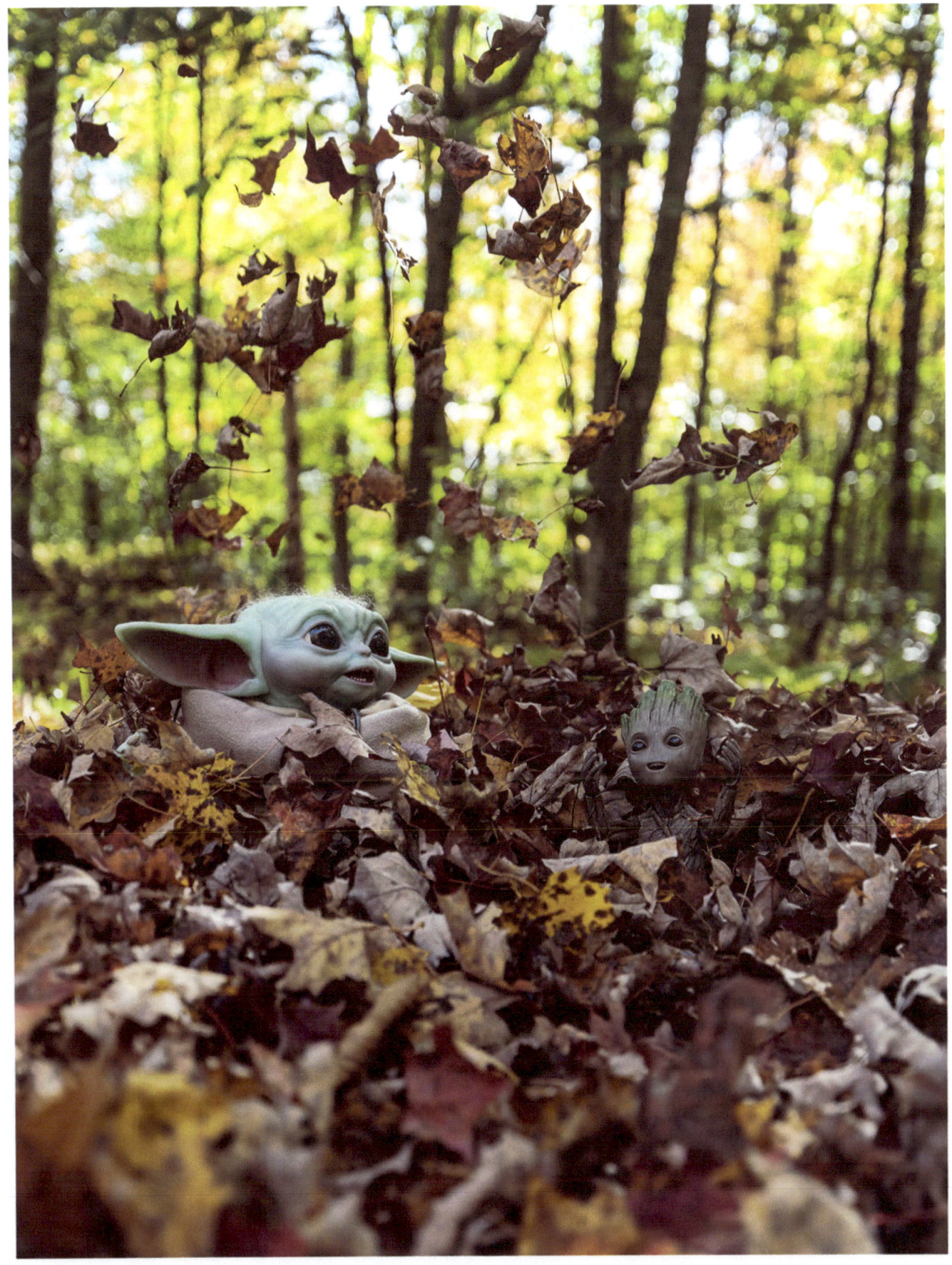

"Falling leaves" - I thought it would be a fun image of Baby Groot and Grogu playing in the leaves.
- **@Northern_fred**

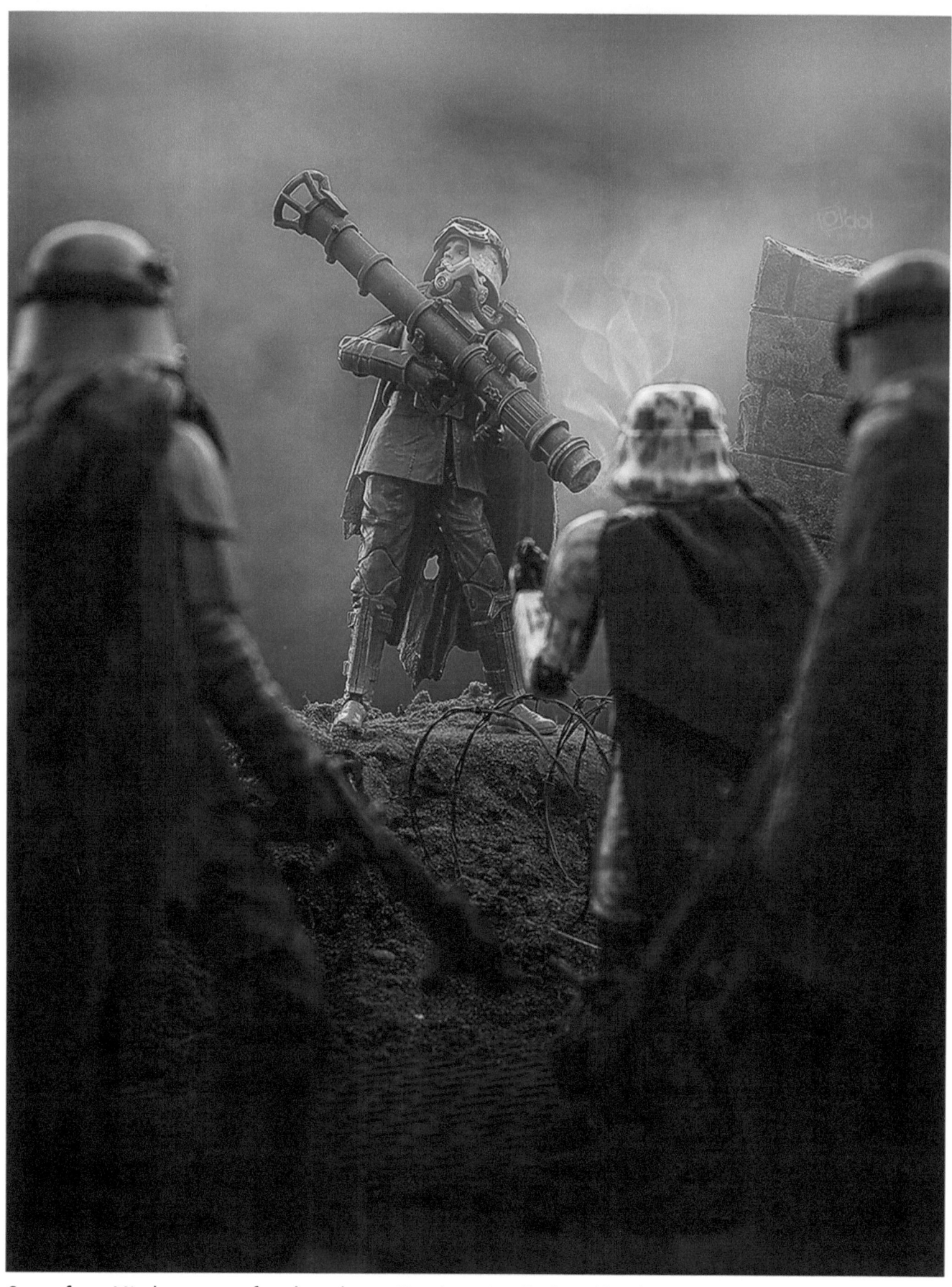

Scene from Mimban - one of my last photos. Toyphoto is still a lot of fun for me. I'm glad this photo will become part of a noble project. - **@odol_studio**

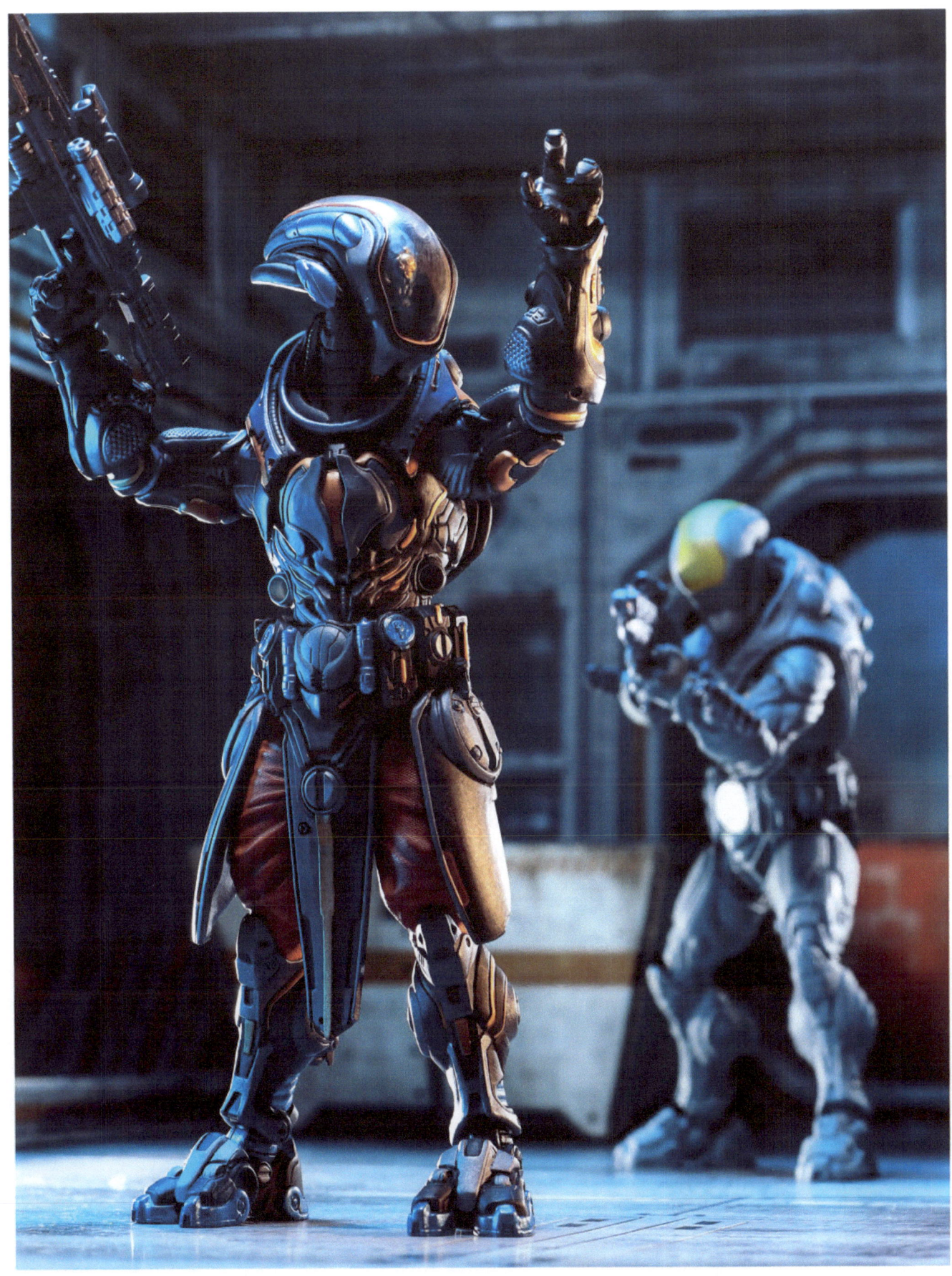

Very happy to be part of the toy photo community to support freedom! Peace! - **@pizzalovermac**

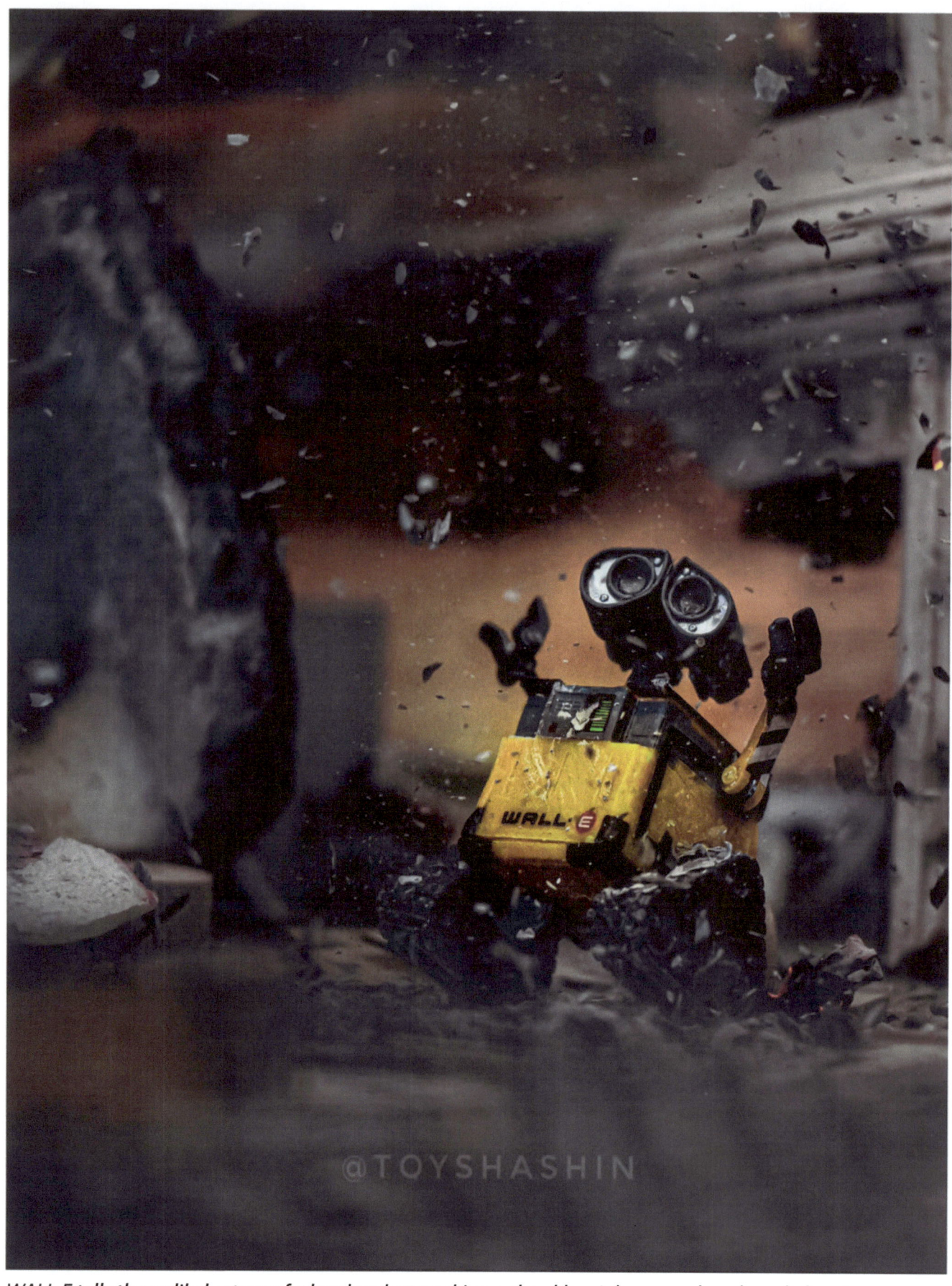

WALL-E tells the unlikely story of a lonely robot working a thankless job on an abandoned planet.
- **@shalizaerna**

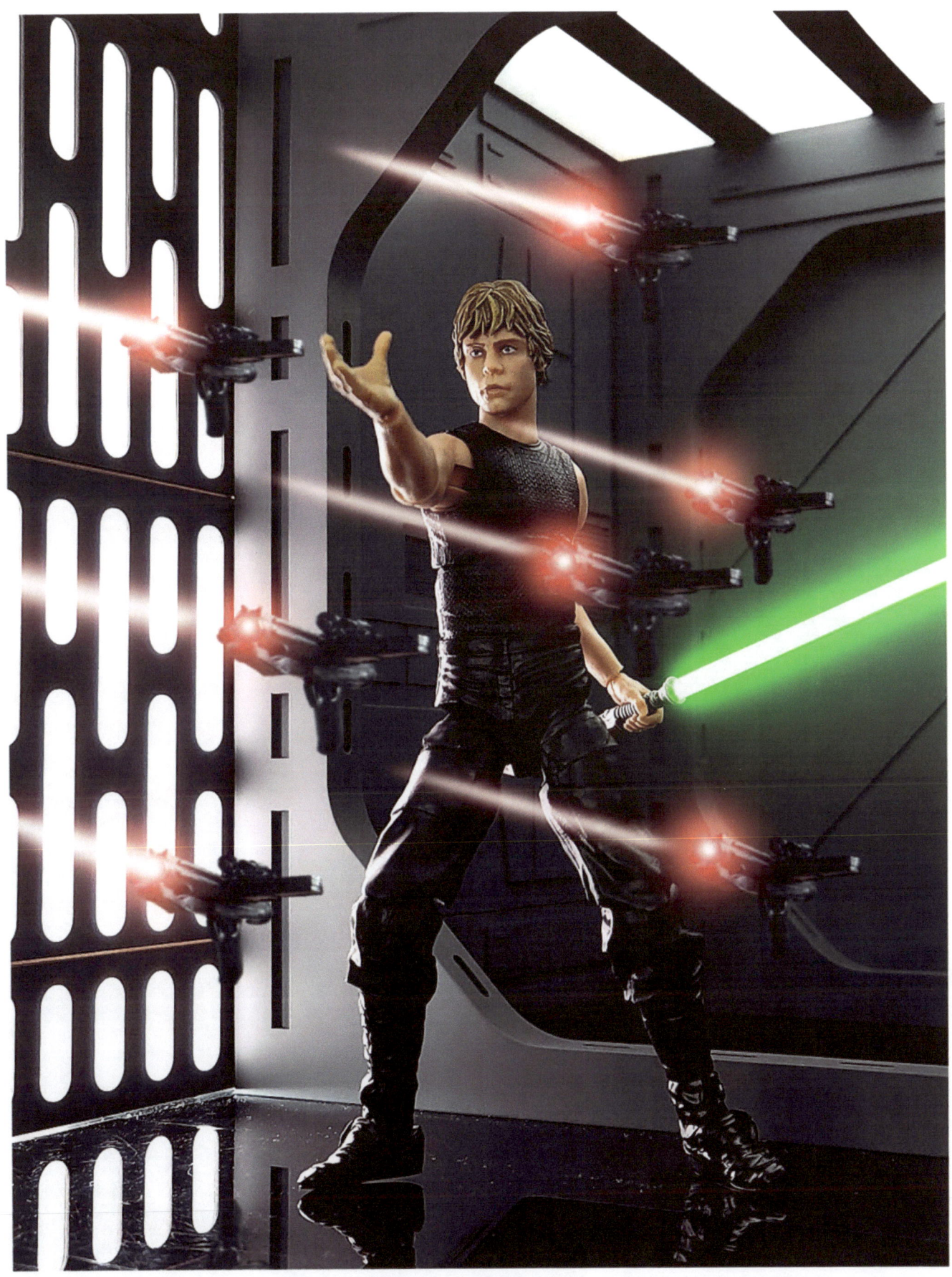

I was inspired in an artwork by Ameen Naksewee, wich features a wounded Ben Kenobi lifting and firing blasters with the force. One day it came to my head the idea to recreate it a bit different, with a master jedi Luke Skywalker, in his full jedi power. - **@starwars_rick**

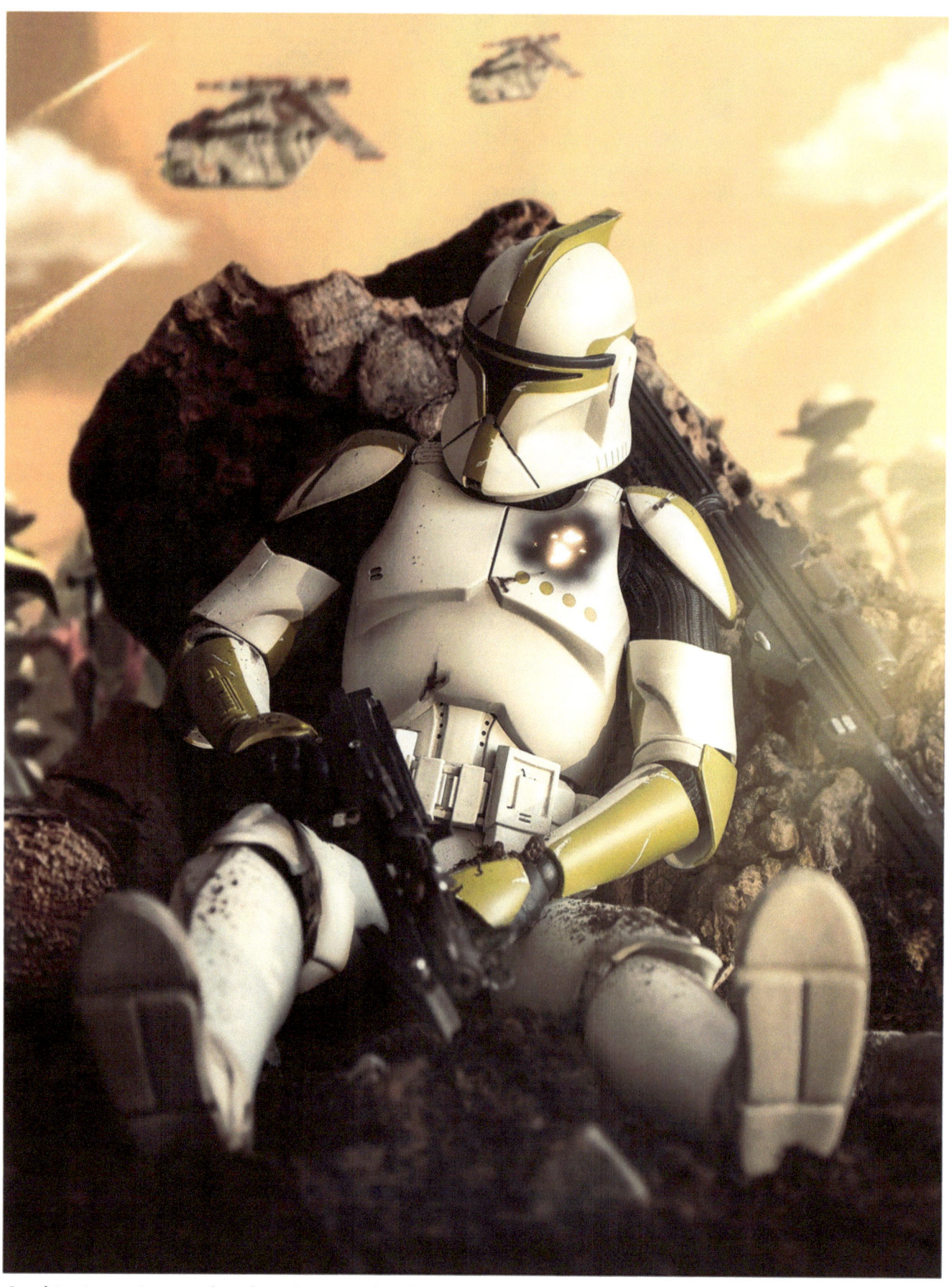

On this picture I wanted to show how cruel and merciless is battlefield. Lonely clone trooper who was waiting for reinforcements didn't make it. He died waiting and guarding his post. He would be proud if he could see how gunships and his brothers are winning this battle thanks to his sacrifice. - @tenks666

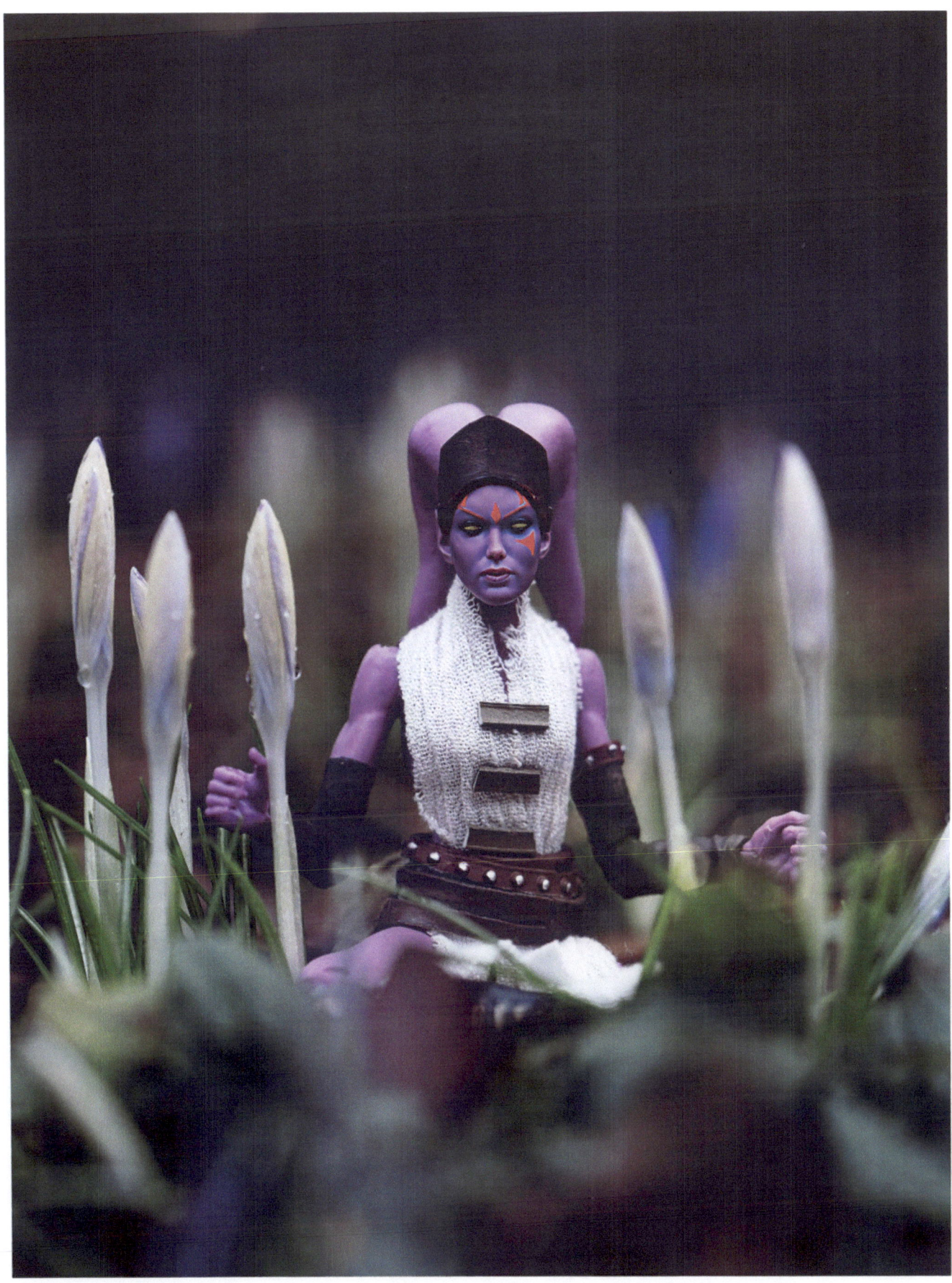

A meditating female Twi'lek. Nature as a temple, tranquility as a pulse and silence as a guide are her companions to the Force.

- @the_m.a.r.co

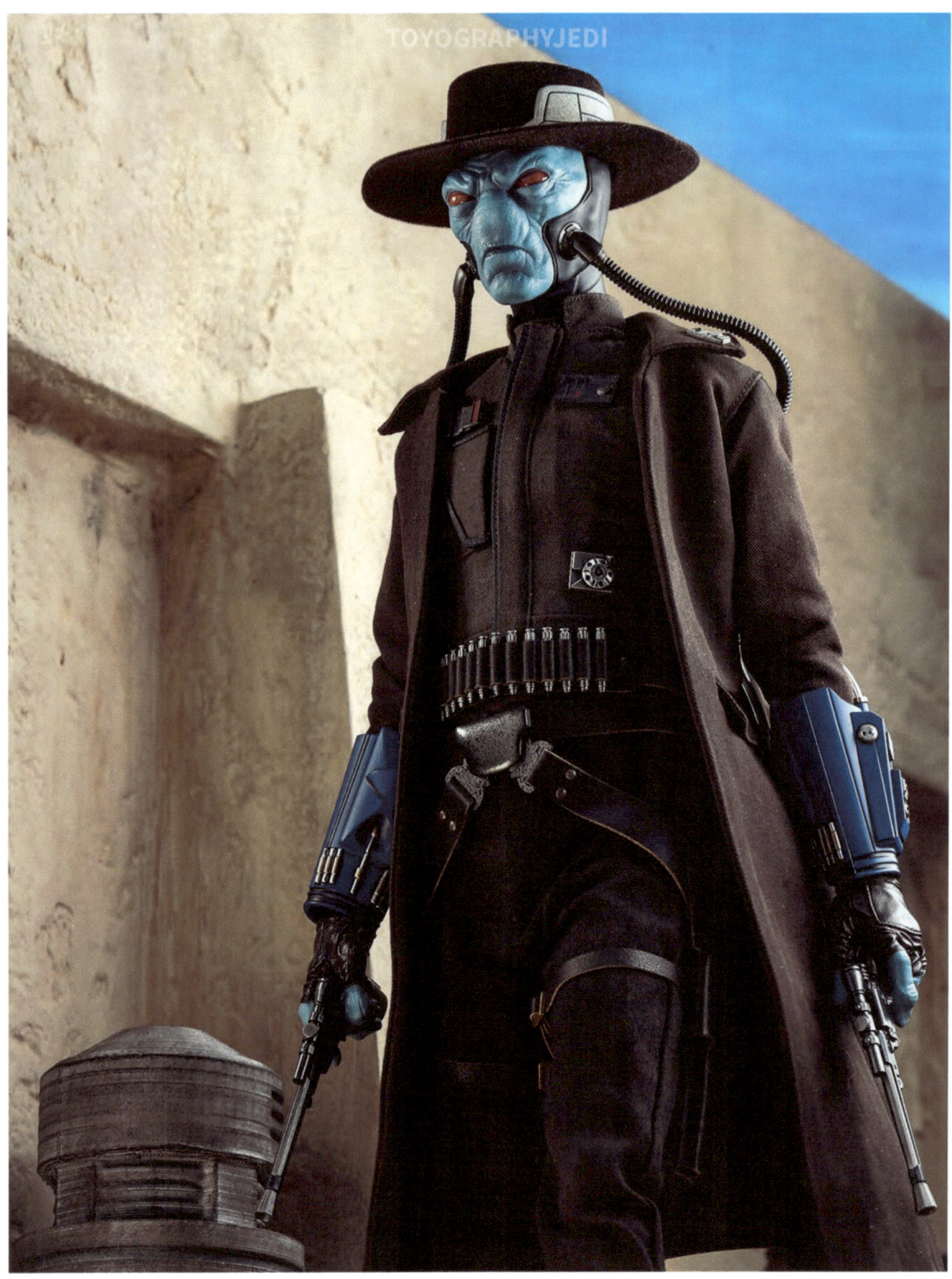

I created the diorama for this shot from scratch and it is one of the biggest dioramas I've created as it's 1/6 scale. As somewhat of a perfectionist I repainted the Tatooine wall close to 4 times before settling on what you see here. - @Toyographyjedi

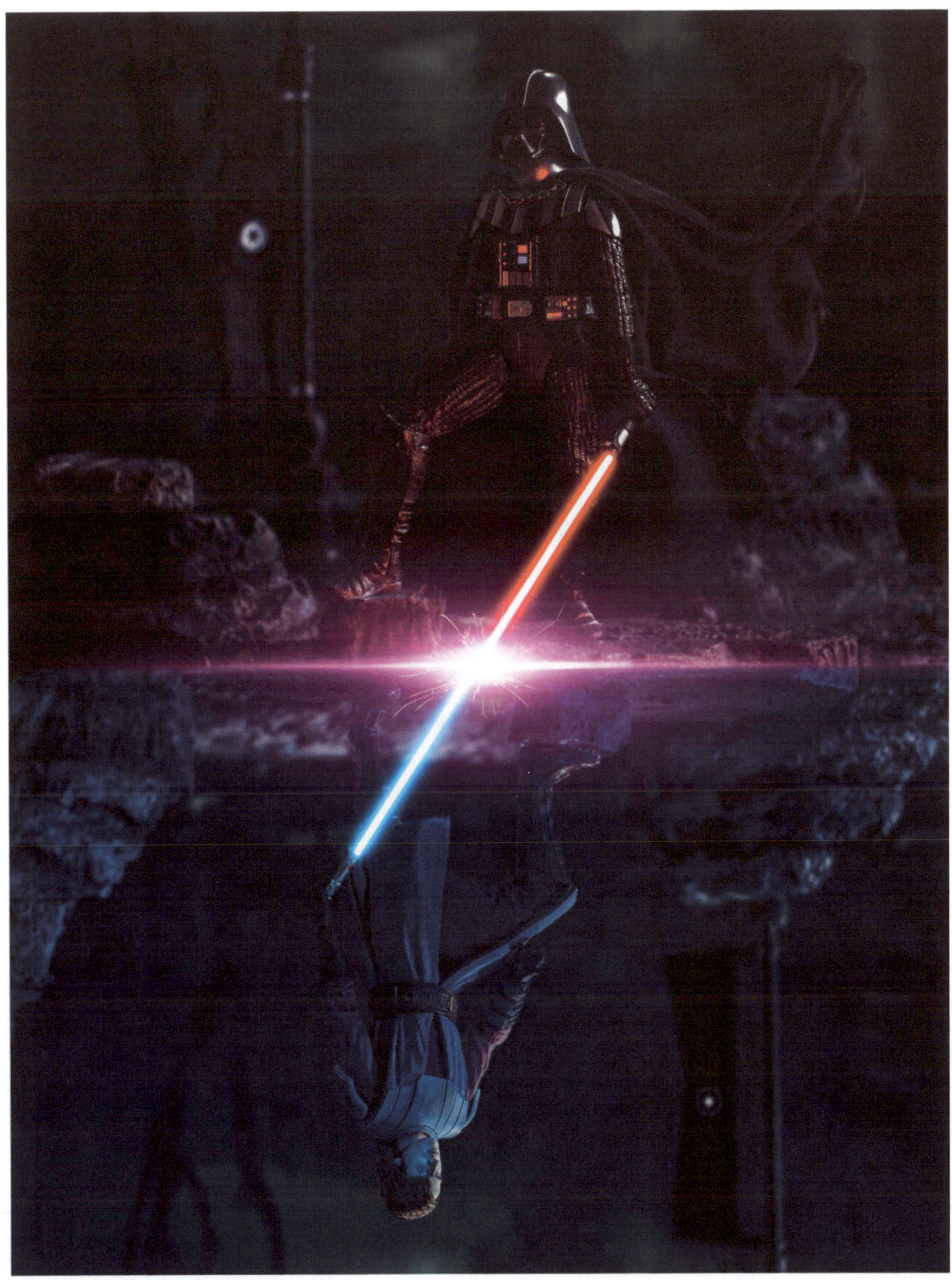

"Duality" - **@UmbraToyPhotos**

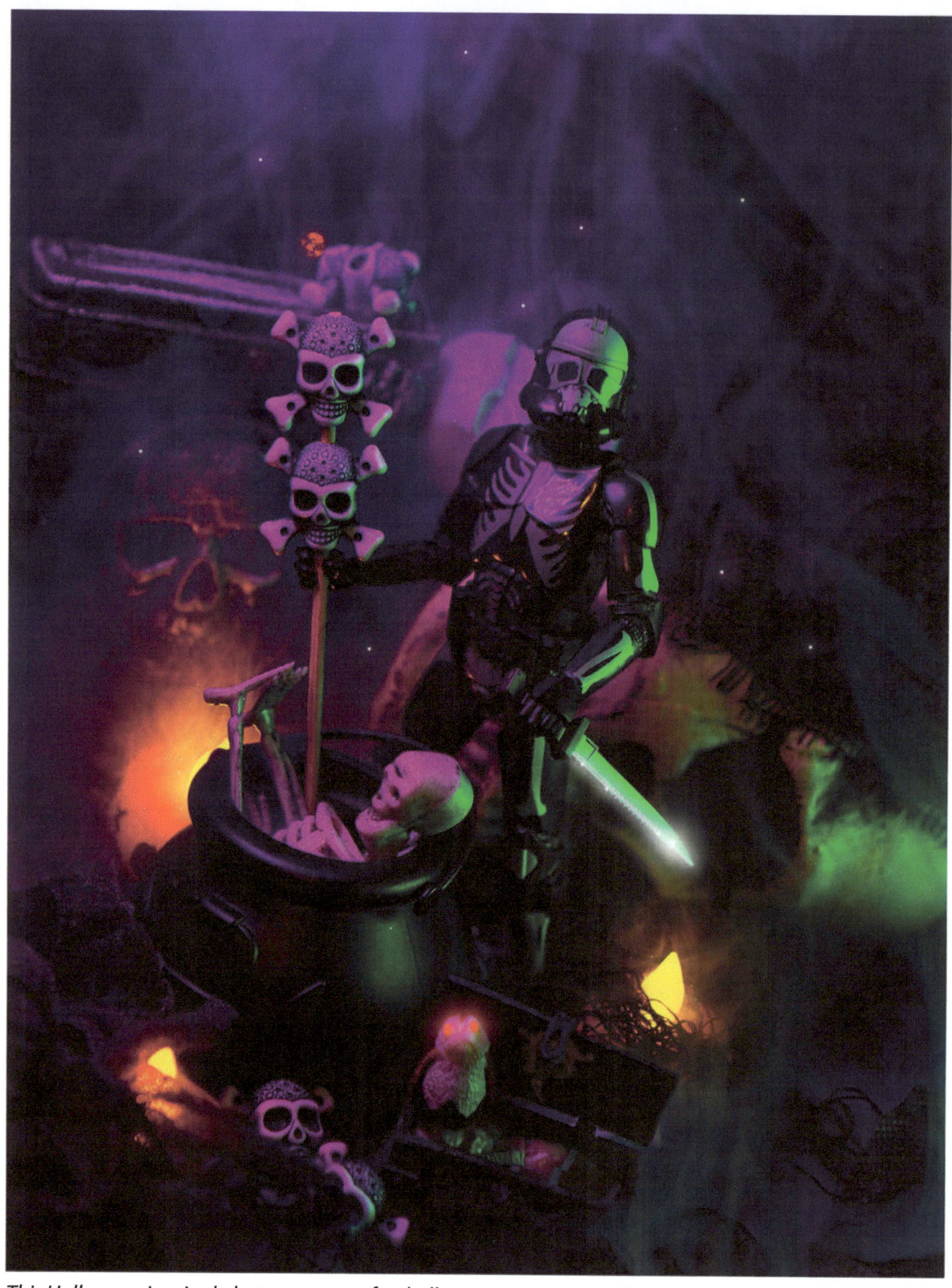

This Halloween inspired photo was part of a challenge to incorporate the number "13" literally or thematically. The photo has hidden Easter eggs, 13 skulls to be found - can YOU find all 13 skulls?
- @wanna_b_like_mike

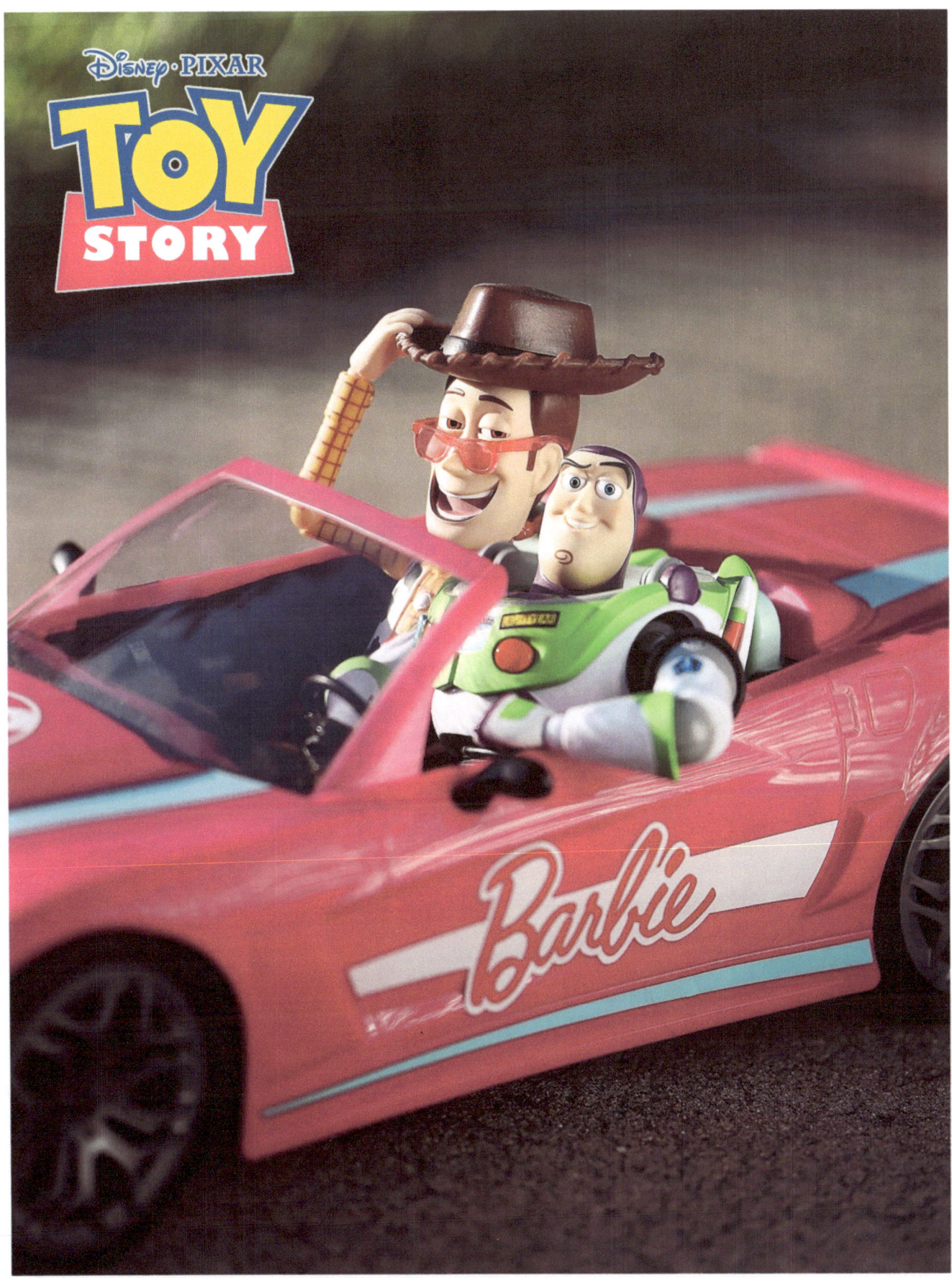

*Inspired by the release of the Barbie movie. I'm also a huge fan of Toy Story. Plus, Barbie was in Toy Story 2. This was perfect. Haha. - **@Wheysnaps***

All profits from the sale of this book go to Médecins Sans Frontières (named Doctors Without Borders in English). It is a charity that provides humanitarian medical care. It is a non-governmental organisation of French origin known for its projects in conflict zones and in countries affected by endemic diseases.

Please donate today: **www.msf.org**